IN SEARCH OF REMOTE HEALTH CARE

BY

NELSON NORMAN

Self-published in 2010 with the aid of:
The Lumphanan Press
5 Auldhill Road
Bridgend
West Lothian
EH49 6PD
thelumphananpress@hotmail.com

ISBN: 978-0-9566149-1-9

Set in Minion Pro

Printed and bound in the UK by the MPG Books Group,
Bodmin and King's Lynn

Jusqu'a la mort on ira.
Resistance motto, Provence.

This book is dedicated to my wife, Morag, without whom none of this would have been achieved.

CONTENTS

Foreword

I WAS DELIGHTED TO BE ASKED TO WRITE AN INTRODUCTION TO NEL-son's latest book, which outlines the development of remote health care in the North East of Scotland over the last four decades. Initially development was sparked by the needs of a fledgling oil industry. It then expanded to a broader global contribution in the remote health care field and now to the new Institute of Remote Health Care.

On the surface this is a history of the development of remote health care in the North East of Scotland, written in Nelson's typically modest style. However, dive beneath the surface and I believe you will find the true essence of the book. It is the characters, the human interactions and the very significant legacy of those initial contributors in remote health care that, certainly for me, create the real story.

Staying with the diving metaphor, and once more moving beneath the surface, there is Nelson's seemingly effortless ability to develop, sustain and work with a tremendous network of people. The players involved surface, disappear out of sight, and then resurface throughout the book. This is no small tribute to Nelson's talent to motivate, and to inspire the impulse to "volunteer". I still vividly remember being in Kepplestone mansion, having only recently returned from the Antarctic. Nelson walked in and casually asked if I had anything planned for the next week. Ten days later I found myself offshore in Madagascar, only returning to Aberdeen three months later. Not an uncommon experience, if you spend time with Nelson.

Looking to the future, Nelson and his team of "volunteers" continue to drive the development of the Institute of Remote Health Care in Aberdeen. This will become the much needed professional "home" for remote health practitioners. There is no doubt that Nelson's vision and persistence will be rewarded and that the very specific expertise available in Scotland will continue to drive improvements in health care in challenging environments across the globe, and indeed beyond it.

Nelson has made it clear to me that this is a more politically correct version than he originally created. However, I think it is quite easy to read between the lines. My advice to readers would be to superimpose your most colourful interpretation of that space between his lines. Even then, it is difficult to consistently match the realities of the time.

Dr Alistair Fraser
Shell International
(ex-British Antarctic Survey and Aberdeen Industrial Doctors)

CHAPTER 1

THE OFFSHORE OIL INDUSTRY
HITS ABERDEEN

Early in the 1970s occasional rumours circulated around the populace of Aberdeen that oil had been discovered below the North Sea. This, as all new information, was greeted with scorn by the average Aberdonian. Everyone knew there was oil in Texas and in Arabia but, even if there was any beneath the North Sea, what did it matter? It had not even been discussed in that source of all North-East knowledge, the Press and Journal. In rapid succession, however, the appearance of a multitude of ten gallon hats in Union Street, American accents in the hotels and restaurants and strange ships in the harbour proved to even the most 'canny' Aberdonian that something was afoot in their midst. The suggestion that in a few years time Aberdeen would be a thriving international centre of the oil industry and could even exceed Houston in importance was greeted with derision. Few realised that the enormous development which was about to happen would change Aberdeen for ever and would require major developments in the medical practices required to support it.

The papers gradually picked up the story and frequently reported on the problems associated with building massive structures in the middle of the stormy North Sea and of the terrible accidents which took place. This was of course in the early days of exploration before the industry had much experience of working in such depths of water and in such a hostile environment. The water in the Gulfs of Arabia and of Mexico is not much deeper than 150 feet, and the sun is nearly always shining. In the northern North Sea the working water depth was between 400 and 600 feet, the water temperature about eight degrees centigrade, and the wind speed and sea state more often at gale force than not. Saturation diving techniques were needed to fix the structures to the sea bed. These were largely experimental techniques, with knowledge of deep diving medicine almost entirely confined to the Royal Navy and the US Navy. Some of the early offshore accidents resulted in horrendous injuries. The management of these injuries far offshore in terrible weather, together with the management of diving accidents, stretched the capacity of the individual practitioners taken on by the oil companies to advise them. The general practitioners involved in the early days of the development of oil company medicine such as Tom Allison and Frank Shepherd were first class and did a great job, but it became apparent that this was a vast and specialist area which would require development. It soon became clear that an entirely new system of medicine was needed.

At that time I was deeply involved in researching and developing techniques of critical patient care. I had spent the previous twenty years in the Universities of Glasgow and Aberdeen combining the practice of surgery with research and teaching. The research had a strong element of cold effects (based on my experiences as medical officer to the British Antarctic Survey base at Halley Bay[1]) and hyperbaric medicine for Glasgow had pioneered the investigation of the use of high atmospheric pressures of oxygen in many disease processes. My interest in cold climates and hyperbaric medicine were well suited to help the fledgling industry in Aberdeen, but I did not quite know how to get involved.

Dr Colin Jones was medical adviser to British Petroleum (BP) and the only oil company doctor resident in Aberdeen. He saw the need for co-ordination and development of the available medical resources and approached the Department of Surgery at Aberdeen university. The reason for choosing my department was that it had been involved in

---

1 See *In Search of a Penguin's Egg*

hyperbaric medicine for the previous fifteen years and was experienced in hypothermia, albeit for surgical purposes. Also, it was currently engaged in research on the care of the critically ill surgical patient which would lead to the establishment of the speciality of intensive care. Diving was the main medical problem facing the industry at first and although industrial diving was carried out at much greater depth than the hyperbaric medicine practised in the Department of Surgery, the physiological basis was the same. Equally, the critical illness research work was leading to the development of techniques that would be needed for the management of accidents which the industry had to deal with, and which were made even more difficult to manage by the time and distance which separated the casualty from hospital. Also, the cold environment posed problems for routine offshore work and in addition to its work on hypothermia the department had experience of work in the Antarctic. It was thus well placed to establish discussion on the type of medical support which would be required.

The relevant senior members of the department were Professor George Smith, head of the department, and me, a reader in surgery. We responded enthusiastically to Dr Jones's approach and agreed to do what we could to help. Colin Jones was full of drive and enthusiasm. He was a big bluff rugby playing Welshman who spoke in short brisk sentences, which emanated competence and clear views. He had absolutely no time for fools, and not too much for those who did not immediately accept his own views either. He had a logical and clear mind, great loyalty to BP, worked very hard and spent what little spare time he had on beer and Tom Thumb cigars. He was like a breath of fresh air in the somewhat stuffy corridors of academe.

Colin was able to provide me with much of the background to the problems and as the only industry doctor based in Aberdeen he had considerable power and control. He had served his early years in the Arabian Gulf and thus knew about oil company medicine and politics. He had experience of diving medicine there – a major advantage – and he had made contact with the Royal Navy diving experts already. He indicated that there was much discussion about the headquarters of the support services for the industry. Both Peterhead and Dundee were strong contenders (indeed Dundee had a large Institute of Occupational

Medicine) but he said his industry had decreed that the base was to be in Aberdeen. Colin and I had many long discussions, gradually developing a rapport and a mutual respect. The early discussions were largely based on the management of diving accidents and the possibilities of transferring diving casualties to the department's pressure chamber in the medical school without reducing the pressure. The possibility of entering a field of interest with the financial help of the oil industry was of course very attractive.

Meanwhile the horrendous and sometimes badly managed offshore accidents continued to fill the newspapers; both the industry and the medical services were criticised roundly. The final crunch came when a doctor, inexperienced in diving medicine but enthusiastic, overruled a very experienced diving supervisor in the case of a diver suffering from a pneumothorax at depth. He insisted that this was a case of pneumonia and demanded that the diver be decompressed immediately. This was done and the diver died. That episode created a very black mark on the quality of Aberdeen medicine internationally – I was furious and felt that something needed to be done to restore our reputation. Further intense discussions between Colin and the department resulted in agreement that the whole problem was so complex that a separate organisation was needed, one that could solve the problem of operating safely on and below the North Sea.

We concluded that the best way forward was to establish an institute to co-ordinate and provide what was necessary. This would have to include the three vital components of any successful medical endeavour – medical service, teaching and research. For that reason we also felt that it would best be placed within the university, but we saw that it would not be easy in the time scale needed. With the best will in the world universities could not speedily establish a new initiative in view of the heavy bureaucracy and committee structure which existed at that time, as well as the shortage of funds and the rival claims and jealousies associated with new initiatives. Also, there were all sorts of organisations which felt that this type of medical support would be worthwhile since it could be both profitable and prestigious. These were not only local companies but large organisations based in commercial outfits, which could move very much faster than a university. Some were based in the States and had the edge on us since Aberdeen's reputation was low following the widely reported diving case.

It was the medical directors of the oil companies that called the shouts, however, and little could be done without their approval. Colin Jones was not the most senior oil company doctor on the scene. He had to contend with the rival claims and ideas of the other companies, chief of which was Shell. The medical man there was Dr Ronnie Houston who was based in London. Ronnie was an entirely different kettle of fish from Colin. He was much more senior and had considerable overseas experience. He was suave, very well dressed, aristocratic and as equally devoted and loyal to Shell as Colin was to BP. Where Colin drank beer Ronnie preferred fine wines (and had considerable knowledge of them). It soon became clear that they were rivals. Indeed, Ronnie rather looked down on Colin whom he considered a brash new boy from a lower class than himself, while the direct Colin considered Ronnie to be a bit of a buffoon – but he was not. Colin had decided that our partnership was worth preserving and he knew that much would depend on whether I was accepted by Ronnie Houston also. We thus had a dinner in Aberdeen, which was a bit strained at first, but it transpired that Ronnie's family had run the Falkland Islands company in Port Stanley, where he had spent much of his early life. A bond was quickly established based on my Antarctic experience and knowledge of the Falkland Islands. It seemed that I was accepted.

It was generally agreed that the institute concept should be promoted by holding a conference in the Aberdeen Medical School as soon as possible. We also felt that experts in the various areas – largely from the services – should be invited to add to Aberdeen's own expertise. In the final discussion we hoped to engineer the conclusion that there was a need to establish an institute. This was billed to take place in three weeks – and in fact it did. The conference was in the main auditorium of the medical school, an impressive locus, and it was packed with participants from industry, service companies, the armed services, government departments and universities.

This was the time that other key players entered the scene, principal among whom were Commodore John Rawlins and Commander David Elliott. They were the naval specialists in immersion hypothermia and diving respectively, and they remained supportive from that time. Naval involvement was virtually assured since we were close to the Medical Director General of the Navy, Vice-Admiral Sir James Watt, who was a surgeon and the department's external examiner. My wife, Morag and I usually had him for dinner when he came to Aberdeen. Indeed the first time we entertained him I spent a fortune on the best vintage port, premier cru class Chablis and 1970 claret, only to discover that the admiral was tee-total!

The other academic involved was Professor Kenneth Donald, Regius Professor of Medicine at University of Edinburgh. He had guided the navy through its underwater personnel research throughout his career and had been responsible for the techniques used by the 'Frogmen' during the war when they attacked the Tirpitz and other German ships in a Norwegian fjord. He was a wise, if outspoken, man who also remained very much involved and supportive. Again he was a big man, not unlike Colin Jones, and just as incisive and highly intelligent. His clear, logical mind made him an excellent chairman.

Despite the short time we had to prepare for the conference it was an outstanding success. Areas of medicine which had been rather specialised before were now of great interest to large numbers of people. With the help of the navy it included a very good symposium of diving and hyperbaric medicine. The management of emergencies was also remarkably well covered because the hospital had a well founded major civil disaster plan. The military members of the medical school provided much useful material as they were involved in the ambulance service and the territorial army. Help was also provided by Grampian Police, who had views on handling major civil disasters that were relevant, and it was good to involve the local community. In the cold climate area our Antarctic experience was also discussed. Several associates and faculty members were involved in mountaineering and mountain rescue organisations, as were the police. The faculty experience in surgical hypothermia was presented but our experience in urban hypothermia, which was more important in the context of the offshore environment, was less complete. Adjacent seats of learning noted that weakness and probed it.

The discussion was brisk and the local expertise was questioned closely and at times a little viciously since there were already several other agencies – academic and commercial, local and distant, British and foreign – which were ready to offer competition to the university. All in all we were pleased with the outcome and felt that the Aberdeen medics and associated community had kept their end up.

The plan was that there would be a final discussion where the case would be made that an institute was needed. There was general agreement on that point because most of the participants wished to be part of such an initiative. Where it would be placed was not touched upon to any extent since it was realised that the oil companies would have a major input. It was fortunate that Colin and Ronnie had decided that the base should be in Aberdeen and that the preferred site was the university. It was fortuitous also that the Department of Surgery had organised the conference and arranged the follow-up meeting with the university hierarchy, because the university still had to be persuaded to accept the challenge.

The meeting duly took place as soon as the conference ended. It did conclude that a special new organisation was required and proposed that it should be sited within the university. The principal – Sir Edward Wright – said it was a good idea and he would be glad to host it in the university, but he warned that he had no money to devote to its establishment. Knowing that the university was strapped for funds a great deal of discussion had already taken place behind the scenes about the ability of such an organisation to make money by providing a variety of medical services for the industry. The presence of such an organisation within the university would provide opportunities for many other departments and faculties. Indeed, when Ronnie Houston asked how much money would be required from the oil industry to establish the proposed institute, Professor Smith said, "None, we do not require marble halls and we will make our own money."

It was thus agreed that a self funding institute would be established within the university. The vice-chancellor still had to take this to the university court for approval and the nuts and bolts of the establishment had to be decided by the university authorities but there seemed little doubt that it would now take place. A major step forward had thus been taken in establishing what was to be the Institute of Environmental and

Offshore Medicine. This happened within three months of Colin Jones's first visit to the Department of Surgery thus indicating that a university could in fact move rapidly if it wished, particularly if it was working in association with a powerful industry.

CHAPTER 2

THE ORIGINAL INSTITUTE

FOLLOWING THE CONFERENCE THERE WAS A GREAT DEAL OF DISCUS-
sion at the university on the establishment of the institute. I had
lived and breathed the subject for several weeks, devoting all my wak-
ing hours to the development and promotion of the concept. Eventually,
Colin phoned me one night to say that the university had decided to
establish the institute but Professor George Smith had said that he would
certainly be the Chairman of the Management Committee and Institute
Director. Colin wanted to know whether I could accept this. This was
a blow to me as I had expressed interest in being director, but I was so
keen on the establishment of the institute that I said I could. I was in
fact very busy since I was still a consultant surgeon with a full clinical
load and with a full schedule of university teaching. I also had several
PhD students and a big commitment to surgical research. George next
appointed the institute secretary who would manage the day to day
affairs. He appointed David Baird, who had just retired from the post
of Executive Dean of the medical faculty. He was a very good man who
had been a colonial administrator previously and had retained his diplomatic skills. He made a good institute secretary.

George Smith was the Dean of the Faculty of Medicine and it had
been decided that the institute would be placed within his faculty, but

he still had to get agreement that it should be placed within the Department of Surgery. There were several other departments that would have welcomed it, such as medicine, physiology and community medicine. The controversial items, however, were usually discussed early on the faculty agenda and the busy and argumentative members usually drifted off towards the end. George waited till most had left and then under the last item – any other business – he said that the university had decided to establish an Institute of Environmental and Offshore Medicine within the Department of Surgery. This was merely for information and the meeting was then closed!

The big medical problem at the time was to do with diving since there were so many diving accidents. It became apparent that a first approach was to ensure that the divers were physically fit to dive. The Department of Energy soon became involved in diving accident investigation and commercial deep diving regulation. It was led by Commander Jackie Warner who insisted on high standards of fitness for divers. We therefore set up a clinic at the back of our hyperbaric chamber in a portacabin and began to carry out diving medical examinations according to the requirements of the Department of Energy. Heaven knows where the money came from to fund this activity but it was organised by David Baird very cost-effectively and indeed eventually provided a small source of finance for the embryo institute. There were still very few doctors who understood the problems of diving but there were enough to carry out this routine activity under Colin Jones's supervision. The doctors in this group were largely those who eventually formed the diving medical team of the area.

This was a good start and was something really needed in service provision. A group of general practitioners then came together under the leadership of Harold Crofts. They not only developed the examinations required for fitness for offshore work but were also prepared to advise on illness and injury offshore. They were also prepared to travel offshore if necessary and to supervise evacuations. They became very efficient in time and provided a good service.

The industry was also concerned about the management of a major disaster which might require the presence of surgical and anaesthetic specialists offshore.

This was the first time the oil companies had worked so close to scrutiny and the media. In other parts of the world they simply built hospitals and staffed them. There was a lot of politics here, however. They were now operating within a highly sophisticated medical community and government had insisted that they used the National Health Service where possible. At the same time it was clear that the National Health Service did not operate below the high water mark and the operators were worried about how they would cope if there was a major offshore disaster such as a fire or an explosion. The interaction between industry, government and the front line health providers was difficult to understand but there was urgency. Colin asked me if I could form up a group of anaesthetists and surgeons with some kit who would be prepared to act if an emergency took place. I agreed and Dr Bruce Howie, who was the Chief Administrative Medical Officer (CAMO) of the Grampian Health Board at the time, encouraged me (quietly) because he knew he could do nothing in view of the National Health Service rules about the high water mark. He also knew that there would be a terrible outcry if there was a disaster and there was no response from the onshore medical authorities.

I therefore gathered a group of volunteer anaesthetists and surgeons together and quietly acquired a set of kit-instruments and disposable items such as drugs and bandages from hospital and theatres. This team was to provide specialist back-up in a major incident to compliment the team of GPs which would provide a first response. There were no pagers or mobile phones so doctors had to be available at home in addition to their normal on-call commitments, and cover had to be arranged for holidays and week-ends. Since there was no budget for this none of these people were paid anything – indeed as full-time university or NHS staff they were not in a position to accept payment. More importantly, however, since they were acting outside their area of contract they had neither personal insurance nor malpractice cover from the health service. All this only became clear after the passage of time. Yet, the devoted group functioned in this manner for far too long. They were thus very vulnerable but accepted the challenge until something more could be organised.

We had a call in the early days when the tail rotor came off a helicopter landing on an offshore structure. It fell off the helideck to a diving barge below and burst into flames. There were divers in the water and the real champion of the event was the diving supervisor who reacted very quickly. He recalled the divers into the diving bell, called the fire service and had the hose on the flaming helicopter almost as soon as it hit the deck of the barge and burst into flames.

When the call came one of the surgeons was having his hair cut and his was the only car big enough to take the box with the Thomas splint. There was an initial delay until he returned and then we could not find the heliport as we had not been there before. When we took off we discussed the problem during the flight but the noise and vibration of the machine and the absence of ear defenders meant that we were hoarse and exhausted when we got there. The next problem was that the security people would not let us off the helicopter because they thought we were the press masquerading as doctors. In any event we had seen a helicopter taking off as we arrived and it transpired that it contained the survivors, treated initially by a team of GPs led effectively by Harold Crofts! Obviously our specialist team needed much more organisation and training, and there was a lot of onshore negotiation and administration to be done.

There was also considerable organisation needed by the onshore authorities because it was not clear where the casualties should be delivered since they were suffering from severe burns. There was no heliport at Aberdeen Royal Infirmary at that time, and the burns unit was in another hospital from the Accident and Emergency Department (where emergencies were normally taken). It soon became clear that a medical co-ordination unit was needed. In any event a beginning had been made to provide for the service needs of the industry but there was a long way to go before an integrated and smooth running system was established. All this did however underline the need for a dedicated organisation to provide for the growing industry, for there were soon about ten thousand personnel working offshore.

The first part of the new medical system, medical service, was initiated however, and it was now time to consider the second element – training – of the three essential parts. Diving was not the only problem; there were certainly many more accidents offshore involving construction workers.

Since they were so far from medical support Colin was anxious that off-shore personnel should be provided with first aid training so they would be able to administer some degree of self help until advice could be provided or medical help could arrive. A first aid course was constructed by the Department of Surgery, which we held in church halls and hotels. First aid was initially described by an Aberdeen surgeon, and indeed the Shephard medal is presented to one of the best final year surgical undergraduates in his memory. The knowledge of immediate care by the present members of the department was not extensive, however, due to the fact that doctors do not have much basic training in first aid. The course needed much subsequent revision, but it was a beginning. Meanwhile horrendous accidents were taking place offshore and the media criticised the industry roundly and often. As far as the third element of the system was concerned – research – it was not possible to make a beginning as we were too busy moving from crisis to crisis.

This was a difficult time for us as we were a busy university department with no extra resources to organise the systems needed. Though I had done my best to get a system organised and knew what should be done I could achieve very little – except the growing displeasure of the oil men at my apparent ineptitude. One of the problems was that there were now so many agencies that wanted part of the action, yet none had the overall knowledge or clout to do much about it. There were several government departments – the Home and Health Department in Scotland, the Department of Energy, the Home Office, the Treasury, the Health and Safety Commission etc. The University of Dundee and the University of Glasgow also made a play but were rejected. The diving industry could do little to get a real grip of the situation because they were contractors to the oil companies and they had no doctors in their employment. The oil companies without medical departments were also powerless. That left Shell, Esso and BP. BP was the only oil company with a doctor who was resident in Aberdeen – Colin Jones. Colin was not the senior man in the BP empire but he was a good politician and soon developed a strong personal position. Shell saw this and appointed Nigel McKay to Aberdeen. Nigel was a good doctor also but he was not the politician that Colin was, and by the time he arrived Colin was entrenched. I had of course formed an alliance with

Colin early on that gave the University of Aberdeen a very strong hold and the opportunity to develop the medical system for the oil and gas industry. It was not clear, however, whether the university was particularly interested in doing so!

A problem that emerged was one of co-ordination of effort. The university and the health service had different agendas and there was a number of professors who wanted to be in charge either for themselves or for the greater glory of their departments. The GPs were their own masters but they looked to the university for guidance and leadership. They also needed co-ordination, liaison with the oil companies and a source of referral for difficult cases. I had seen all this and was being pushed into it by Colin Jones, but I found it increasingly difficult to direct since although we had the institute I did not have the benevolent support of my senior academics as Colin had in the industry. One of the problems was that a university could not respond rapidly to a need for innovative behaviour. In these days they were unlike commercial organisations since they had so many committees and cumbersome faculty structures. The industry wanted things to happen fast. After some thought and further frustrations I asked Colin about the possibility of initiating some sort of organisation like a company, which could take its own decisions and act like a commercial organisation – albeit still an academic department. His view was that a company could certainly be set up easily but would be no different from all the companies springing up all over Aberdeen. The university connection and access to the NHS facilities were essential.

At that time there were no university companies and the only connection that universities had with industry was in the form of the odd charitable contribution or contract for a service rendered. They still rather looked down on commerce in much the same way as the eighteenth century aristocrats did. The discussions continued, however, and it seems likely that Colin took advice from Matt Linning, whom he regarded very highly and who had just been appointed as general manager of BP in Aberdeen. Matt was a very bright Glaswegian who personified the tough, outspoken face of Glasgow. He had no frills and certainly called a spade, 'a bloody shovel.' He epitomised the classical characteristics of the erudite Scot.

Eventually Colin invited me to accompany him to a meeting at the New Ventures Department of BP in London. This was a department which BP used to diversify some of its profits into new ventures such as fish farming and forest development. We spent the day in Brittanic House in the city of London with Roger Newton. He was a pleasant man who though bright had the ability to put one at ease immediately. I explained our problems and suggested the possibility of setting up a kind of autonomous company hopefully within the university. I felt we were struggling to establish a new mini-speciality of medicine which was not only important to the industry but which had great potential for the community and overseas development. I stressed the importance of keeping the academic activities of teaching and research together with the thrust of medical service if the initiative was to attain its potential within a reasonable time-scale. I also said that the venture was very capable of making a profit but that pure commercial profit was not the primary aim. I hoped that any profit made could be ploughed back into the academic side so that we would not only be running a first class medical service for the industry but establishing a self-funding university department. He questioned me in great detail for most of the day and when Colin and I retired to our hotel for dinner Colin seemed quite delighted with my performance. He had made the introductions but left me to do the talking and only commented from time to time. I felt I had done my best and realised that there would be much consultation before we heard anything further. Unlike a university, however, answers came through remarkably quickly.

A great deal of talk apparently took place in London and there was discussion with the other major companies such as Shell and Esso. Finally, the university was approached and out of all these discussions the company known as Offshore Medical Support was born. It was one of the first university companies.

The company had four oil company directors and three university directors. The Chairman was to be a BP man so that BP had two directors. Professor George Smith was appointed a director, with the other university directors being Max Gaskin, Professor of Political Economy, and Calum MacLeod, a lawyer who was a member of the university court. Matt Linning was Chairman and the other oil company directors were Colin Jones, Ronnie Houston and Peter Swann of Esso. A general manager was required and in the event a BP secondee, John Hughes, was appointed.

This seemed a good move at first but it transpired that it had also been agreed that the concept of medical service, training and research was too ambitious and the company would concentrate on medical service only. This destroyed the concept worked out carefully over the previous year and was very disappointing for those enthusiastic about the academic potential of the institute. It was suggested as a sop that the company would concentrate on making money and that would be used to fund the academic remnant of the institute, which was now in effect a separate entity from Offshore Medical Support.

CHAPTER 3

OFFSHORE MEDICAL SUPPORT

IN THE 1970S ABERDEEN WAS LIKE THE YUKON DURING THE GOLD RUSH. It had been converted from a quiet, market town where the main economy was based on fishing to a noisy bustling international cen-tre where everyone seemed to be jostling for part of the action. House prices soared and hotels and boarding houses mushroomed. Air traffic increased enormously and a new airport was begun to replace the green wooden hut at Dyce – but the Aberdonians clung tenaciously to clos-ing the airport at 20.00 hours sharp for many years. A new heliport was built and Mr Alan Bristow filled it with Sikorski helicopters, which were now common sights over the city.

Life changed fast in some areas but not in others and the latent entre-preneurial spirit of the Scot became manifest. There was a couple who made a modest living from buying wood and arranging it for kindling. They saw the great shortage of space which was developing and invested in a couple of porta-cabins which were sold for a great profit, instantly allowing the purchase of several more. Soon they had the market cor-nered but did not depart far from their original rather frugal practices. The business had a meteoric advance in size and the story is told that they were visited by a couple of oil executives negotiating a massive order for porta-cabins. In the midst of the discussion they were offered a cup of coffee which was accepted. As they were leaving a tin was produced from a desk drawer with the expression, "That will be twenty pence each for the coffee. Just put it in the tin."

When John Hughes was appointed as general manager of Offshore Medical Support (OMS) there had been two possible candidates. His rival was Steve Dick, who was about to retire from his post as a principal in the Home and Health Department of the Scottish Office. Both were good men but though John Hughes had considerable experience in running a company he had no experience of working with the NHS, universities, or government departments. Steve Dick was a master negotiator in all these areas but had little knowledge of the oil industry at that time. John Hughes was chosen and when Steve Dick retired he went to the North Sea Medical Centre in Great Yarmouth and looked after its development in the Southern Sector of the North Sea very effectively.

The first thing John Hughes had to address after his appointment was the construction and equipping of a medical building. Despite his lack of medical knowledge it was a remarkably good and functional building; John achieved it rather well and within a reasonable time and the allocated budget. It was, however, hardly surprising that the next problem was political, arising just after the building was complete. The Foresterhill site in Aberdeen, where both Aberdeen Royal Infirmary and the University of Aberdeen Medical School are sited, is jointly owned by the National Health Service and the university. The land which the OMS building used was on that part of the site which was regarded as university land. The unions, which were very militant at that time, picked this up and made a great fuss about a private medical facility being on a site partially owned by the NHS. This was a much more serious matter than it would be now because Michael Foot was leading Labour and there were a great many of the far left-wing in the party. The papers were full of it and the oil companies were displeased because of the negative publicity. The university and the leaders of the NHS were not best pleased either. It was just one problem after another, but though it seemed real enough at the time it was all sorted out suddenly and quite quickly – probably since oil was so important to the nation's economy.

At about the same time the insurance company General Accident established a rival concern called Gaelic Healthguard in the city, put Admiral Stanley Miles in charge and offered a full range of medical support for the oil industry including training and research. Admiral Miles had been in charge of the Institute of Naval Medicine and was a well known authority on remote medicine, diving and the recently researched aspects of resuscitation at sea. He was also a friend of Professor Smith, who had invited him to lecture at the university on several occasions. The admiral had a very fine office in a very prestigious building in the west end of Aberdeen but was not welcomed into the university community as he expected. This was sad as he was a fine man who could have been very useful. Also, he was offering the full triad of the original institute concept – medical service, training and research. Since Shell and BP offered no more support than the university General Accident closed his operation down a few months after it was established. He was of course in direct competition now that OMS had been established so he could really expect nothing else. It is likely that the industry had considered using his organisation, which was well staffed and had much potential, but it had been found wanting in some respect by them, so it was doomed.

It was becoming clear that real competition to OMS would not be tolerated. By this time several groups of GPs were providing both routine and emergency services for the offshore industry. The main one was that well organised group led by Harold Crofts. Since it was popular with the contracting companies and there was no readily available alternative the OMS directors wooed it, taking it over so that they provided their services through OMS. They carried out the routine pre-employment and periodic medical examinations for fitness to work offshore and they provided a rota for emergency calls, giving advice by telephone and also being prepared to travel offshore if necessary. OMS provided some of the equipment and looked after them well, providing insurance cover, medico-legal cover and marketing. They were provided not only with a place from which to work but were supported by efficient nursing and administration, together with the increasingly important provision of litigation insurance since a large number of Americans were now involved. Doctors outside the cartel were discouraged and the practice at Peterhead and the North Sea Medical Centre under Robin Cox in Great Yarmouth were not encouraged to extend their efforts to the Aberdeen area.

As we began to grasp the principles of practicing remote medicine, we found one of the key requirements to be a co-ordinated group of doctors that understood the problems of the offshore environment, were available twenty-four hours a day, experienced in communication with remote areas and were prepared to travel offshore in emergencies. Such a group was now being established and the best service for the industry at that time was by such an integrated and co-ordinated group. All were amateurs but the group was learning fast. The top-side system, as it was called to distinguish it from the diving problem, was thus reasonably well taken care of.

John Hughes now turned his attention to the support of diving. He took over the clinic already established in the institute and housed it in OMS. Some of the topside GPs had taken an interest in diving and were keen to be involved also but it was recognised that knowledge and experience were needed even to examine divers for fitness to dive. The only course available was that conducted at the Institute of Naval Medicine for new entrant naval medical officers. It was run by Commander David Elliott, who had become very interested in the deep diving practices of the industry and had discussed the organisational problems often with the institute in Aberdeen and with the diving industry. Ultimately the Navy agreed to take a portion of civilian doctors on its introductory course in diving medicine. This was funded by Shell, courtesy of Ronnie Houston. The course was only designed to prepare doctors to examine a diver for fitness to dive but it was soon insisted by the authorities that all those practising diving medicine should have completed it successfully, even though it did not provide sufficient knowledge and experience to manage diving accidents well.

For routine diving medical support John Hughes wanted to set up a group of diving doctors who would function in much the same way as the topside doctors, however it was a different problem. The group he attempted to recruit were GPs, oil company doctors, NHS personnel and university staff. A main administrative problem was that although John was very anxious to have a diving medical team drawn from all four medical backgrounds only the GPs, as private contractors, could be paid. The rest were full time employees of the university, the NHS and the oil companies and thus could not be paid. Most would happily have provided their services free of charge since they were really interested in diving medicine, but junior doctors were not well paid in those days and it rankled to see the GPs creaming off large sums of money when the rest got nothing. This was a recipe for disaster. Mike Childs, one of the university doctors who later decided to devote his career to diving medicine, was particularly vociferous. He was very articulate and almost went to war with John Hughes. The creation of a two part organisation was thus already causing problems as the academic and the purely functional and commercial aspects began to clash.

As far as it went OMS provided a reasonable medical service. However, it fell far short of the potential which it had for the industry, the community and the university. It was not a particularly happy organisation and although most of the needs of the GPs were met John Hughes was not popular among the doctors. The management of a group of doctors is not an easy task since they are trained to have one-to-one relationships with patients and have strong views of their own on both management and ethical principles. They always need a leader who is either a doctor or someone with a profound understanding of the principles of medical practice if they are to act as a loyal and co-ordinated team. While there were a couple of doctors on the OMS board they were not involved in the day to day running of the company.

It was not clear why but BP decided to withdraw John Hughes and deploy him to the direction of another new venture project. The post of general manager was thus advertised. The ideal candidate would have been Steve Dick but he was already established in the North Sea Medical Centre company at Great Yarmouth. The board decided to appoint David Webster, who had been a manager on an offshore related company. It was felt that he would really understand the needs of the industry. That was perhaps so, but the job was actually about managing a group of doctors. He greatly impressed the university group at his interview, however, with his enthusiasm and vitality. He expressed the importance of the original institute concept and the need for research and development in training, and in the management of remote medical problems. Someone must have given him a copy of our original writings on the subject. Unfortunately it soon became apparent that he had the same problem as John Hughes in that he did not understand the principles of medicine. He also had little respect for doctors, something that no amount of enthusiasm or managerial ability could compensate for.

The main initial problem, and that which the whole world concentrated on, was the underwater environment and the health and safety of deep divers. They were a close knit and very professional group who attracted much admiration as they were essential to the wealth of the nation and risked their lives often. It was a privilege to be involved in their medical care.

The difficult diving medical problems of the 1970s were dealt with by a group that came together in the hyperbaric unit of the Department of Surgery, led by Colin Jones and I. This 'committee' provided integrated medical advice from sources which were both local and furth of Aberdeen. Ready support and advice was available from John Rawlins and David Elliott from the outset and both provided unstinting backup through the difficult years that followed. Tor Nome from Stavanger was another committee member as was Commander Jim Vorosmarti from the US Navy. The cases were thus managed by this local committee rather than by an individual doctor and the difficulties were overcome effectively. The necessary external support was established early depending on the nature of the problem. Tor Nome remained in association for several years. He was a great friend of Colin Jones and a bit like him physically. He was much quieter, however, much more polite and much more diplomatic. He also gave much confidence in his medical opinions.

There was a case during a winter storm when we had a report of a diver north of Shetland who had been struck on the head by a piece of angle iron which someone had dropped from an offshore installation. He was recovered into the offshore chamber but was exhibiting bizarre neurological symptoms which mystified the 'committee' in Aberdeen. We took advice from consultant neurologists and also from diving specialists in Portsmouth and the States but no-one could work out the significance of the signs – nor the big question of whether he should be decompressed in case he needed a neurological operation. Eventually we decided that one of us would need to go and examine him but we were advised that the weather was such that we could not possibly get to the rig. The storm was, however, passing from west to east and the weather people suggested, with tongue in cheek, that if we had been in Norway we could possibly have made it. We phoned Tor who jumped into a helicopter and made the rig in the nick of time before the whole North Sea became storm bound. Some time later he reported back that he had no idea of the neurological diagnosis but he was confident that the diver did not need an operation. That was basically all we needed to know so we all went home to our beds. Poor Tor, however, was stuck on the rig and had to wait till the storm abated.

It was a year before the diagnosis was eventually established. He was a malingerer seeking compensation and there was nothing wrong with him – indeed the angle iron may never have hit him. There were no scans in those days, and it was only discovered when he was leaving the out-patient department with a terrible gait problem and someone looked out of the window to see him hopping easily into his car!

That was not the only time when the importance of the Norwegian connection proved to be of value and it showed again the need for a medical organisation which was co-ordinated. The offshore structures were largely mid-way between Norway and Scotland and this could be important in managing the evacuation of emergencies. There was a major neuro-surgical unit in Aberdeen but none in Stavanger, so it was important to evacuate serious head injuries here rather than there.

In these early days saturation diving was barely out of the laboratories and the diving industry did not have much experience of it before it was required to become operational in deep waters and a hostile environment. The routine was that divers entered a large pressure chamber mounted on an offshore structure and were compressed to the simulated depth of the dive work-site using a mixture of oxygen and helium (air is narcotic at depths greater than fifty metres). They remained at the same atmospheric pressure for the duration of their work-cycle – usually a couple of weeks – and when they went to work they entered a diving bell which took them to the work-site. When they finished their shift they re-entered the bell which conveyed them back to the pressure chamber. At the end of the work cycle they were very slowly decompressed over a few days.

This was a relatively safe form of diving and decompression sickness was not common in the Aberdeen practice. The big problem, however, was access to the diver if he became sick from a routine problem like appendicitis, trauma or chest infection. The main subject that always arose was the management of appendicitis – divers were in the appropriate age group in which it usually occurred. As there were about a thousand divers in the North Sea it thus seemed likely that appendicitis would occur sooner or later in saturation. It could take several days to get a diver out of the pressure chamber if he was sick, and little was known about decompression techniques in sick people. It could also take a doctor about a day to get into a chamber at, say, a simulated depth of six hundred feet, and he would be unlikely to be much use by the time he got there from possible neurological consequences of the deep oxy-helium environment. At first it was felt that the best bet would be to determine a way of transferring the casualty from the offshore chamber to the onshore facility. The difference in pressures was such as to require another chamber of much greater depth capability, which meant that there would be a need to transport the transfer pressure chamber. Would it be by sea or by air? Helicopters had a limited weight capability that was greater than the conceived design of possible transfer chambers together with their life support apparatus. A ship on the other hand would probably take too long in an emergency. Even when the ship docked the diver would still need to be transferred without changing the pressure to the hyperbaric unit at the medical school. This difficult discussion continued over several years and got very heated at times.

In addition to the problems of compression the divers were maintained in very unusual environmental conditions because helium conducts heat six times faster than air. When the divers were in the water they were bathed in hot water to provide the heat which they lost from their breathing. The reduced density of helium also made it very difficult to communicate with them since they spoke like Donald Duck! With each case treated, however, the group gained experience and confidence. The routine examinations of divers for fitness to dive were being carried out in OMS, which was making money now. The doctors were gaining experience there also and were managing some of the emergency cases. The complex cases were still managed by the 'committee' in what was known as the institute, but there was a growing need for research as more and more problems were identified which needed practical research to solve. The problem was that we had no money.

A major advance was made, however, when one of the GPs phoned me about a terrible diving accident. A Comex diver, Derek Bannister, had been explosively decompressed from a depth of eighty metres when the counterbalancing weight of his diving bell came off and it shot to the surface. His buddy diver died and Derek sustained desperate injuries to every system of his body – including paralysis from the neck down – but he was just alive. He had been recovered into the offshore pressure chamber and Drs Iain Macauley and Nigel McKay had rushed offshore to enter the chamber where they had managed to keep him alive during decompression. Iain Macauley phoned me and asked me to take over his care when he came ashore. This was both a very difficult medical and political task.

The Comex doctor, Dr Xavier Fructus, based in Marseilles, was a very experienced diving medical specialist. He had rather unconventional views with which the Royal Navy did not agree. A previous Comex diver had come under the care of a Royal Navy doctor – Lt Commander Tom Shields. Tom had violently disagreed with Dr Fructus and had applied to his ultimate boss, Vice-Admiral Sir James Watt, Medical Director-General of the navy for support. George Smith happened to be in the Admiral's office at the time and could do nothing but support Shields. This caused considerable problems thereafter. When Derek came ashore from his diving ship Colin and I had made plans to rush him to the hyperbaric unit at the hospital with a police escort in very early morning when the streets were empty, but I was met at the gangplank by Dr Fructus and the French contingent and asked who would be in charge of the further management of the patient. I replied that since he was to be admitted to a National Health Service Hospital that I would be in charge – since I was a consultant of the National Health Service. I also said, however, that I should be delighted to have Dr Fructus's help and advice and that in fact we would manage the case together. This was acceptable and Dr Fructus and I became friends thereafter, together managing this very complex case. Though paralysed from the neck down and with almost every system of his body severely damaged we saved his life. But we could not recover function below the middle of his back. It was quite remarkable that we did obtain recovery of the function of his upper body, however.

Many people were involved in this case, including at least ten consultant specialists. Mike Childs, who was a Senior House Officer in surgery, became very involved. He sat with the patient for almost the whole six weeks of acute care in the hyperbaric unit and alerted the team on the almost daily crises which occurred for the first few weeks. I carried out a tracheostomy in the pressure chamber. The anaesthetist was another young man, John Ross, who became fascinated with diving medicine. He was a close friend of Mike Childs and they both determined to devote their lives to diving medicine. John went on to become the director of the National Hyperbaric Centre many years later but Mike unfortunately died before achieving his full potential. We felt our way through the case by using the basic principles of medicine and physiology and when it was eventually presented to the Royal Navy diving doctors they were impressed. Commander Ramsay Pearson stated that there was no way they could have achieved what had been achieved in Aberdeen. David Elliott was also present, who by this time had become established in the North Sea as a diving consultant. I was pleased and felt that Aberdeen medicine had now recovered its reputation following the early diving accident that had led me to attempt to set up an institute with Colin Jones. Indeed, when a highly regarded diving manager and former diver from Texas, Bob Boylestone, said at a meeting that he would rather be looked after in Aberdeen following a diving accident than anywhere off Houston my pride knew no bounds.

CHAPTER 4

DIVING MEDICINE IN THE INSTITUTE

THERE WERE MANY PRACTICAL DIVING MEDICAL PROBLEMS WHICH needed urgent attention but the institute did not yet have the resources to become involved with the necessary research. Equally, research takes time even if funded. The diving industry was impatient and also becoming more and more concerned about a lack of co-ordinated medical support for divers in Aberdeen. The industry had set up a group called the Association of Offshore Diving Contractors (AODC) but since they had no medical input they looked to the medical authorities in Aberdeen to provide it, and it was felt that this was lacking. Malcolm Williams, co-owner of the diving company Wharton Williams and chairman of AODC, called a meeting in the Skean Dhu hotel of all the diving company chiefs and doctors he could think of – including the navy doctors, David Elliott and John Rawlins. Colin Jones and Ronnie Houston were invited along as were George Smith and I. Malcolm was loudly outspoken about the apparent failure of the doctors to set up a proper co-ordinated system of medical support in Aberdeen. George Smith came in for a considerable amount of criticism and Malcolm almost demanded that a medical committee was established which would report to and liaise with AODC. There was a little money available for the support of meetings and it was agreed that a liaison officer would be appointed from the AODC to act with the proposed committee. Malcolm asked Rear Admiral John Rawlins if he would be willing to take this on and chair it. Admiral Rawlins agreed immediately and Malcolm then asked Colin Jones, David Elliott and George Smith to take part. Outside Aberdeen he invited Tor Nome and Nick McIver from the North Sea Medical Centre at Great Yarmouth.

The first meeting of the diving committee duly arrived and as luck would have it George asked me to represent him because he could not go. I was both surprised and delighted and I turned up at the inaugural meeting of the committee, which was duly entitled the Diving Medical Advisory Committee or DMAC. The admiral was a strong chairman, used to command, and since there were so many naval officers on the committee he was not often overruled. He ran the committee very well. He stated the matter to be discussed and then asked the opinion of each man by name round the table. In this way everyone had a clear chance to offer an opinion. He then allowed a short interactive discussion before authoritatively summing up. One of the points under discussion was, of course, liaison with AODC. Others were the post of secretary and the organisation and management of the committee. The representative from AODC said that he would write the minute of the current meeting but could not manage to do it subsequently. He did agree to organise the meetings and to liaise with AODC, however. Since there was no money to pay for a secretary and everyone on the committee felt that they could not devote the time required for the job that problem was not resolved.

When the second meting of the committee took place it transpired that George again could not go so he asked me to deputize. Once again I was surprised and pleased and took a full part in the discussion. At the end of the meeting the question of who was going to be secretary arose once more and since everyone had a good excuse for not taking it on I offered to do so. My offer was immediately accepted with gratitude. On the way out David Elliott whispered to me, "Looks as though you have cracked it." I wondered about this and about what George would say when he heard. I decided not to tell him immediately and indeed I had not reported back on what had happened in detail at either meeting. Some kind soul did tell him, however, before I got round to it and he was absolutely furious. He accused me of failing to keep him informed and abusing the position he had given me. I had a sneaking feeling that he had a point but I was keen on the DMAC position so I just kept my head down for a while!

The institute had in fact responded to the problem of managing diving incidents during the seventies, doing a very good job in spite of difficult circumstances. In retrospect it is not clear what Malcolm Williams was getting so worked up about. Equally, AODC had a bit of a cheek requiring so many senior people to devote time and travel in forming a committee to co-ordinate its activity when they could not even consider supporting it to the extent of providing a secretary. AODC was fortunate that there were so many devoted people in the navy, the oil industry and the university who were so keen to help.

Meanwhile all sorts of other agencies were taking an interest and considering how they could get into the action. This was probably because the media could think of little else. There were so many accidents in the North Sea – both above and below the waves – and everyone seemed to have an answer for sorting things out. Dale Falconer, Secretary of the British Medical Association in Scotland, came to Aberdeen about this time and spent a day discussing the problem with me. He would have liked me to suggest that the BMA should set up a committee to take over the direction of things. I did not agree and suggested that it would be better if advice was taken from a government committee which the Secretary of State for Scotland might set up. I also suggested that a good chairman would be Professor KW Donald who had just retired from the Regius Chair of Medicine at the University of Edinburgh. This was partly in view of his lifetime of work in diving and his current chairmanship of the powerful Royal Navy Personnel Research Committee. I also knew that his ideas were along the right lines since I had visited him on several occasions and he had taken a major part in the conference which had resulted in the establishment of our institute. I also suggested that he should involve the industry and named both Colin Jones and Ronnie Houston.

Diving was still the main problem, which meant that the navy should be represented. John Rawlins was now in charge of the Institute of Naval Medicine so he was an obvious choice. Commander David Elliott was equally important in view of his pre-eminent position in diving medicine and his strong interest in the North Sea industry. I was therefore quite pleased when a few months later Bruce Millin, who was then Secretary of State for Scotland, announced that he intended to set up a national committee to advise him on what action he should take to improve health care for the offshore industry personnel and all these names were included. This became known as the Donald Committee. Indeed, I cannot remember anyone else on the committee making much of a contribution apart from Professor Boucher, the Professor of Medicine at Dundee.

I received an invitation from Ronnie Houston to join him before the first Secretary of State's committee meeting in Edinburgh at the Shell House in Herriot Row. It was in the same street as Robert Louis Stevenson's home and was a very fine place, fit for the directors of Shell to use as their Edinburgh pad. The other guests were Admiral Rawlins, Colin Jones and David Elliott. This was now the core group which promoted much of the future direction of offshore medicine in the North Sea. It transpired that Admiral Rawlins had just been promoted to become the Medical Director-General of the navy with the rank of Vice-Admiral and Ronnie wanted to have a private party to celebrate this with some fine champagne. We were all delighted with this development because the navy was so important to our cause and had a very high profile. Also, to have the MDG of the navy on our side was a big plus point. We repaired for lunch to a marvelous French restaurant. We then duly turned up at the inaugural meeting of the Secretary of State's committee a full twenty minutes late. It was held in the prestigious New St Andrew's House and I seem to recall that we were not very apologetic even though we had kept the under-secretary of the Home and Health Department waiting to open the committee!

Professor Donald's Chairmanship of the committee was a little different from the Admiral's style with the DMAC but there was steel in his manner. He was determined to steer it towards diving and only diving. Steve Dick was still a principal senior servant at the Home and Health Department at this point and was appointed to service the committee. A very senior man such as that suggested that the committee was regarded as having considerable importance. Steve had the diplomatic manner of the senior civil servant and was enormously efficient. The whole committee got on well with him and Ken Donald was particularly impressed, which said a lot because he was certainly not easy to impress. Everyone on the committee was invited to submit papers on the areas which they considered most important for the attention of the Secretary of State. Since diving was still a considerable problem and very much in the public mind it was reasonable that it should have first attention, though I was beginning to feel that it was now being coped with rather well. Nevertheless, a persuasive case was being made from several directions, led by Ken Donald, for the establishment of a deep hyperbaric facility somewhere in the civilian sector. This would be capable of carrying out any treatment at depth that might be required, as well as catering for present and future training needs. It was decided that a meeting in Portsmouth was required so that the whole committee could see what was entailed in such a hyperbaric facility. We duly met at the naval dockyard in Portsmouth and were provided with a very clear picture by the naval and civilian personnel involved there.

Steve Dick came along and got very interested in the whole scene, to the extent that Admiral Rawlins invited him to become a member of DMAC, to which he became a useful addition. It was an astute move by the admiral since Steve was obviously influential in the Scottish Office, close to the Secretary of State's committee and had become really interested in the problems of diving. The committee met several times in Edinburgh and there was much discussion – with a bit of territorial wrangling – about where the facility should go, but it was tacitly agreed that a major hyperbaric facility was going to be recommended. The main discussion was on how far to go. It seemed pretty obvious that it should be located in Aberdeen and I did not need to lobby very hard on that point, nor on the insistence that it was a complex of at least three independent compartments which would allow research to take place and yet maintain one chamber constantly on stand by for the reception of a patient.

Did we need an adjacent ward with nurses and did we need an animal facility for research and how much extra equipment and personnel were needed? These were the main discussion points. Eventually the report was completed – very well argued by Donald and Dick. The Donald report is still regarded as the standard for what is needed in hyperbaric medicine. It was not long after its submission that Bruce Millin accepted it without argument. We were all delighted but it was a long time before the recommendation was implemented.

The successful management of the serious diving medical problems of the seventies had put Aberdeen on the map as a competent clinical diving support area. It was now time to devote effort beyond medical service to the other tenets of this new medical endeavour, namely training and research. The Royal Navy introductory course in diving medicine for new entrant naval medical officers was, however, massively oversubscribed. This was partly because sport diving had become increasingly popular and diving was no longer confined to naval establishments. Also, doctors now felt that they might be called upon to treat a diver wherever they practised in the country, since divers did not normally live in Aberdeen. They only came to east coast areas to work. Doctors had also become aware of the possible commercial opportunities which such knowledge provided. Equally, diving was now taking place in many overseas locations as exploration for oil gathered momentum and the supporting doctors of these operations required training.

I discussed the problem with David Elliott, who was as helpful and friendly as usual, and we decided to run these courses in Aberdeen with his help and advice. Before this, however, I felt that institute personnel should attend the Navy's course so John Smith, Mike Childs and I duly signed up and were welcomed to the Institute of Naval Medicine in Portsmouth by David Elliott. In addition to an excellent course we were shown all sorts of related training areas that the navy provided but which were not generally known about, such as submarine escape training and the training schedules for navy divers.

In order to demonstrate the narcotic effects of nitrogen and the physical feelings of pressure for those who had not experienced them before we were compressed to a simulated depth of fifty metres and given some simple tests of mental arithmetic. I was mortified because John Smith got all his right and I – the consultant and his boss – got most of mine wrong! On another day they showed us a great column of water which they used for various test purposes, such as submarine escape training. The instructor told us that there was a breathing set we could use if any of us wanted a shot at diving. Ronnie Cumming, the consultant surgeon at the Gilbert Bain hospital in Shetland, was desperately keen to have a shot. He was helped into the SCUBA apparatus and immediately jumped into the water. The problem was that no-one told him that you had to be able to swim before you took up diving!

The effects of cold are also important in diving, since both helium and water conduct heat away much faster than air. Commander Frank Golden, who lectured on this subject, was a leading expert on immersion hypothermia. The difference between the applied and the theoretical aspects of medicine arose when Derek Johnson, the charismatic GP from Stromness in Orkney, asked how you would manage a case of immersion hypothermia in a drunk man who had fallen into the sea at Stromness and was taken into a local cottage. The commander had emphasised that it was important to re-immerse the casualties with warm but not hot water and gradually to increase the temperature of the water. "And what do you do", said Derek, "If there is only a tiny hot water cylinder in the house?" The commander paused for thought and Derek said, "I'll tell you what you do: you fill the bath with all the hot water in the cylinder and then you immerse the casualty in it." "That would be so painful that he would immediately jump out," responded the commander. "That is why you have to jump in also to keep him there!" said Derek. The fairly large group from the North-East indicated the interest and importance which was felt in the subject there. They acquitted themselves well, were down to earth, thoughtful and outspoken but jolly good practical doctors. We now had doctors with a knowledge of diving extending down the east coast from Shetland and Orkney to Aberdeen and beyond. They looked towards Aberdeen and the university as their academic home. I was anxious that we should be worthy of that position and worthy of their trust.

We now set about offering our own course in Aberdeen. Initially we had some help from the navy[1] but we were soon running the courses ourselves – although one of the naval diving doctors usually came up to help. This was the only course in diving medicine outside the navy so we were soon fully subscribed with doctors from all over the world

1 In particular David Elliott through the Institute of Naval Medicine, which had Admiral Rawlins in charge. The admiral allowed others to assist also – particularly Lt Commander Tom Shields.

attending. Gradually the institute became the recognised training school in the civilian sector of the nation.

As time passed and the institute's confidence developed David Elliott suggested that we should establish an advanced course in diving medicine, one which would produce doctors with a real knowledge of diving and the management of its medical problems. This was an ambitious project since diving facilities were required for the practical work. The first course was held at the underwater training centre at Fort William. It went well, so we were encouraged to continue and held the next course in the Comex facilities at Marseilles with the famous Dr Xavier Fructus.

On the basis of diving medicine the second element of the system, training, had been established firmly. Fees were charged for these courses and this gradually helped the institute to become self-financing. It was now possible to consider the third element, namely research. The institute research development was added to my area of responsibility and so I merged it with my existing surgical projects. The university then decided to appoint me to a personal Chair of Environmental Medicine, which underlined the establishment of an enlarged research endeavour. I was ably assisted by two young surgical colleagues, John Smith and Mike Childs, who had been very much involved in the care of Derek Bannister, and had helped with the organisation of the initial specialist teams designed to act in the event of a major incident offshore.

The research required had gradually evolved as problems were identified during the service and training work. The attraction of a self-funding department was that it was possible to initiate relevant research of practical importance and interest without the necessity of persuading elderly London academics to fund it. The early promise of financial support from the commercial activities of OMS was not forthcoming but the institute was now developing its own funding stream from training. The concept of a self funding university department as a model apparently now seemed possible.

One of the first problems we found was that some divers were becoming unconscious at depth for no identifiable reason. This was taken up by Mike Childs and a grant was obtained from the Department of Energy to pursue it. This was complex problem that occupied the group for many months. John Ross, the young anaesthetist who had been involved in the management of Derek Bannister, had also begun his involvement in hyperbaric research and he obtained support for fundamental research into a new area of the study of action potentials at depth.

An immediate practical problem was, however, the diagnosis of chest pain in pressure chambers. This always caused alarm bells to sound following the dreaded case of misdiagnosed pneumothorax in the past. The pain may be mild, but it was nevertheless always worrying. This came into focus when there was such a case and Colin Jones once said with real feeling, "If only we could get a chest x-ray or sound the chest from outside a real advance in diving medicine would be made". When the next case of difficult chest pain presented Mike Childs took a small, discarded, portable x-ray machine that he had found in the basement of the offshore installation infirmary and took an x-ray through the port-hole of the chamber. It worked. On that occasion it was clear that there was no pneumothorax but that there was air around the diver's neck. When an attempt was made to decompress him the air expanded and compressed the great blood vessels in his neck. The lung rupture was central – a condition known as mediastinal emphysema. Mike had also brought an electronic stethoscope which was attached to a plug that penetrated the wall of the chamber. This allowed the diver to place the bell of the stethoscope on his chest while the doctor listened outside. With further development these two pieces of kit worked well and constituted a major advance in saturation diving medicine with particular reference to the vexed problem of the diagnosis of chest pain.

This first case of mediastinal emphysema occurred reasonably close to the surface. Since there was no advice in the diving literature on how to treat the condition we played it by ear, waiting for an arbitrary three days for the rupture to seal then decompressing the diver very slowly under continual medical supervision within the chamber. The second time there was a similar case the diagnosis of mediastinal emphysema was made offshore by taking the x-ray in the support vessel that housed the chamber. This time the diver was at the equivalent of 400 feet depth and it would have taken more than a week to decompress him if he was perfectly normal. This created major medical, ethical and commercial issues which we will discuss in the next chapter.

The institute was now approached about all sorts of problems. Colin Jones came one day, for example, because there was a sudden outbreak of ear infections in the saturation divers of several companies. All divers have ear infections which respond to drops and clear up if they dry their ears and look after them. This was different because they were really sick and in so much pain that the dives had to be aborted. The cost of aborting a saturation dive was in the region of one hundred thousand pounds per day so the problem was urgent. I approached a young bacteriologist called Steve Alcock and we were duly transported to an offshore installation. We examined the divers' ears, took swabs from them and thoroughly swabbed the chamber, pumps and other equipment. There was no evidence of infection anywhere in the chamber complex but we grew an organism called Pseudomonas pyocyaneus from the divers' ears. This is a very nasty bug commonly associated with burns and not often seen in ears. It likes salt water and seems to flourish at raised atmospheric pressure. In other words it revels in the environmental conditions commonly found in saturation chambers where it seems to increase in virulence. On decompression it becomes quiescent but remains in the ears for at least ten days. It is sensitive to antibiotics but antibiotics had no effect in controlling the infection at depth. The eventual answer was to screen the divers at the beginning of a dive so that pyocyaneus was not admitted to the chamber, to reduce the humidity as low as possible and to keep the divers ears as dry as possible. This worked well and the bacteriology department made a lot of money from the diving company Comex, both in research terms and routine service from screening.

On another occasion a young geneticist, Brenda Page, came to see me saying that she routinely examined any saturation diver whose offspring was born with some sort of defect, such as six toes or a cleft palate. She had only collected ten cases but she had found chromosomal abnormalities in all and they were more marked if the diver had been diving for a long time. This was obviously a bit of a time bomb that could have had massive consequences for the development of the resources of the North Sea – if there was anything to it. I discussed it with David Elliott who agreed that it should be kept under wraps until it could be investigated, but we would need to be very careful not to conceal it for too long. A senior government official needed to be in charge so I phoned Jackie Warner, who was in charge of the Department of Energy Inspection Team. When I put him in the picture this resulted in an immediate massive research grant to Professor Forbes Robertson's genetics department in the university. The whole thing was conducted in great secrecy for some years and even I could get no inkling of the results found. Finally, it emerged that there was indeed chromosomal damage in divers but it was of the order of magnitude of that caused by smoking twenty cigarettes a day. During this investigation it was also pointed out that divers were much more likely to father daughters than sons. I noted that Antarctic explorers also frequently fathered daughters. This was taken into account by the complex epidemiological investigation conducted by the genetics department but it was found that there was no substance to these statements. And so another environmental theory bit the dust!

These were two examples of work commissioned for the university with considerable financial advantage for its research funding. It was good to be in a position to further general university research even though funding did not come the way of the institute. It did, however, justify the initial claim that the establishment of the institute within the university would result in research advantages for a variety of departments.

A lady doctor from Turkey, Maida Kimsit, obtained an academic attachment to the institute at that time. She wished to carry out research in a diving related subject leading to an MSc by research. She decided to compare the lung function of divers who smoked with divers who did not smoke. Against all pre-conceived ideas she could detect no deterioration in lung function in divers who smoked compared with those who did not, at least until they were well into their thirties. She was very keen to gain access to the diving facilities of Portsmouth, but when the commander responsible was asked for permission he said there was no way a foreign national would be given access to the naval dockyard. She was a very beautiful lady, however, with the most amazing green eyes. I suggested that she approach Admiral Rawlins during a diving conference in Luxemburg. Later I noticed her speaking to the admiral and so drifted past. The admiral was gazing into her amazing green eyes and saying, "The facilities of my entire navy are available to you, my dear."

CHAPTER 5

THE NATIONAL HYPERBARIC CENTRE

THE NATIONAL HYPERBARIC CENTRE HAD A DIFFICULT BIRTH. FROM what seemed straightforward following the Secretary of State's acceptance of the Donald report, the hiccup was that Andre Gallerne, the chief of an American diving company, wrote to the Scottish Office and offered it a very large and rather old hyperbaric chamber. This was surplus to his requirements, a single compartment chamber and not nearly as good as the complex which Aberdeen had just been awarded by the Secretary of State. Gallerne was anxious to see that the transfer chamber, or hyperbaric stretcher, which he had produced was available and used. Since it was built of titanium it was now just within the maximum weight which could be accommodated by a Sikorski helicopter. This would give Gallerne some measure of commercial advantage in the competition for diving contracts since the oil companies were anxious to show that they were safety conscious and liked to demonstrate their concern for the care of the personnel for whom they were responsible.

Initial discussions between Colin Jones and I had been on the question of the feasibility of transferring a sick diver to a shore based chamber without changing the pressure. We had debated this approach intensively and were now not at all sure whether transfer under pressure was the best way to manage diving illness. I had been making the point for some time that if a patient deteriorated and needed urgent intervention while in a one man transfer chamber all that his attendant could do would be to watch him deteriorate further and possibly die.

The solution favoured by Colin and I was for a group of trained specialists to travel offshore and to be with the patient while he was decompressed and taken ashore. If he suddenly ran into trouble – such as by the rupture of a perisplenic haematoma or respiratory obstruction following a chest injury – he could at least be given a chance of survival, even though it was not the optimum place to administer an anaesthetic or carry out an operation. BP had funded an institute project to examine the feasibility of establishing a mobile intensive care unit.

There were eventually three cases of appendicitis in saturation chambers while the institute was responsible for diving medicine in the North Sea. They all resolved without incident by using the conservative regime which had always been used twenty years before if the history was of more than three days duration. It was known as the Oschner–Sherren regime, but powerful antibiotics were added. It also worked well in the two cases of appendicitis which occurred (in a decade) when I was in charge of the British Antarctic Survey Medical Unit.

The Gallerne chamber created all sorts of problems because a single compartment chamber was by no means ideal for the management of deep diving illness. This act of Gallerne, while the best means of managing diving illness was still under active consideration, allowed him to counter the government's previous position that since the National Health Service did not operate beyond the high water mark the management of deep diving illness was thus a matter for the diving companies. By producing his transfer system he could now say "Here is a sick diver in a small chamber above the high water mark – deal with it!"

With the state of the nation's finances at that time the Scottish Office had little alternative but to accept Gallerne's kind offer and send the chamber to Aberdeen. When it arrived I was invited by Dr Bruce Howie to determine what should be done with it. This was a National Health Service initiative but until then hyperbaric medicine was in the provenance of the university. An NHS committee was thus established by the Grampian Health Board with me as chairman to advise the board on how to bring the chamber into use. In the short term the Gallerne chamber was placed in a warehouse at Dyce, five or six miles from the hospital, and we had to set it up as a kind of mini-hospital with appropriate stores and support. Technically, it was operated and maintained by Dan Walker – a good man on Andre Gallerne's staff, on a contract to the health board. The titanium transfer chamber was retained by Gallerne but the contract for its operation was awarded to OMS. The committee was left with bringing into commission a kind of intensive and specialised care unit several miles from the main hospital, which had to be able to cater for all sorts of hyperbaric emergencies. In this welter of contracts and high finance the only unpaid part was my self-financing university department as usual!

There was an increasing number of problems which still needed urgent research appraisal. It was still not known how to administer an anaesthetic safely in a pressure chamber, the answer to why divers sometimes became unconscious underwater had not been solved nor how long a diver would survive without heat if the umbilical cord to the diving bell was cut, or even how to decompress crushed tissue after an accident. The appearance of the Gallerne chamber virtually wiped out the planned programme of practical research since the single compartment chamber had to be kept empty and in readiness for the reception of a possible patient.

Meanwhile, it was considered that the Gallerne chamber was just sufficient to cope if a diver had to be treated before the definitive complex was provided. Quite a number of sport divers were received who had been diving on the scuttled German Grand Fleet at Scapa Flow in Orkney. Scapa Flow was a bit deep for tourist SCUBA divers, who were sometimes unfit, but they pushed their luck and often ended up suffering from some form of decompression sickness – often the serious spinal type.

There was also the second case of mediastinal emphysema referred to before. This case occurred at the equivalent of 400 feet depth and it would have taken more than a week to decompress the diver if he was perfectly normal. It was a clear case for transfer under pressure because the barge was on a lucrative contract and the cost for each day out of service was in the region of three hundred thousand pounds. The commercial pressure to remove the diver by transfer under pressure (TUP) was thus intense from the diving company and the barge company. I was also rather in favour because I wanted to try out the system in a case where there was little likelihood of deterioration. Mike Childs was totally opposed to it, since he foresaw risks in using an untried system and we had a great argument on the barge which had come into Peterhead. I eventually pulled rank and the diver was duly loaded into the transfer chamber and transported by road to Dyce and to the chamber. I had to go to Newfoundland next morning and left Mike Childs in charge. He took six weeks for a very canny decompression but the diver made a good recovery. As far as I know that was the only occasion when the system was used for the transfer of a sick diver.

The third case of mediastinal emphysema was many years later, the diving ship once again coming into Peterhead. This time the diver was at a depth of less than a hundred feet and we had a good x-ray facility at Peterhead. By that time there was a roster of nurses trained in diving techniques. I again considered transferring him under pressure but had come to the conclusion by that time that these cases could be managed better by just waiting a couple of days for the tear to seal then decompressing them on the saturation mode while under careful monitoring. This ship was also anxious to return to sea but the captain had to wait for a replacement bit of machinery so I was given a maximum of four days to get the chamber cleared. I placed a specially trained nurse in the chamber who could provide a flow of information. After a couple of days the diver was slowly decompressed by about twenty feet and examined again, with more x-rays taken. There was no sign of deterioration so the procedure was repeated a few hours later. Then the diver was decompressed in the normal saturation decompression mode. The diver was fine and the chamber was cleared just in time for the ship to sail. A reasonable method of management for mediastinal emphysema had thus been established which satisfied both medical and commercial criteria. It also avoided the risks of using the TUP system.

The argument about the place of TUP in the management of deep diving accidents continued, however, becoming quite ferocious and international. It was now show-down time and the DMAC decided to resolve the argument finally by holding an international conference of all the interested parties. Ronnie Houston agreed to host the conference which took place in Shell Centre, London.

Admiral (now Sir) John Rawlins was in the chair. American specialists and diving companies were there, as was the Department of Energy and its diving chief, Jackie Warner, the Royal Navy, the US Navy, the government and the oil industry. Commander Ramsay Pearson was doing his first secretary job – he did not have a problem with the minute because I think the admiral had already written it before he came! It was all most impressive. From where I was sitting I could see Big Ben out of the window, and such a picture always makes one feel that one is at the centre of things. The admiral, as usual, arrived just after the meeting was due to begin and was therefore last. In a body the officers of the Royal Navy rose to their feet. The rest of us were thrown into confusion; some rose half-heartedly while the Americans did not really know whether they were coming or going! The admiral thus had command of the situation and though we all tried to give an opinion he did not brook any deviation from his own – and presumably from the report he had already written. One thing I will say about Ronnie Houston is that he was an excellent host and everything was of the finest at Shell Centre. At about a quarter to one Ronnie said, "I think if we proceed to the dining room at this time the Montrachet will be just about the right temperature when we get there" – and it certainly was. I cannot remember the final outcome of the meeting but I am pretty sure it did not make much difference to any of our views. It was probably the view expressed by Addison's famous character, Sir Roger de Coverley, "There is much to be said on both sides."

CHAPTER 6

AN INDEPENDENT INSTITUTE

THE ESTABLISHMENT OF OFFSHORE MEDICAL SUPPORT LTD WAS AN excellent and far-sighted move, particularly at a time when commercial companies were rare in academic institutions. It could have been the ideal base from which to develop the self-funding institute. Unfortunately, its structure was flawed from the outset. That had implications which delayed the emergence of the original institute concept by more than a decade. The central cause of the problem was the decision that OMS should confine its activities to the provision of medical services for the oil industry. It was to be a commercial organisation, its function was to make money to fund the academic part of the institute and to make a financial contribution to the university. Medical service, training and research needed to be developed together in the same organisation if the new form of remote health care was to develop as planned and in a reasonable time-scale. In effect the format chosen for the inauguration of OMS created two separate entities which were housed in two separate buildings with two management structures – one classical academic and the other commercial.

OMS was housed in a purpose built structure and managed by a commercial business man while the academic part remained in the Department of Surgery. Professor Smith was the medical man responsible for both parts. He was the only university doctor on the OMS board but he held such a variety of posts that it is not clear whether he attended many meetings. If he did there certainly was no feedback to the remaining part of the organisation. In any event OMS was run by its general manager under the influence of the powerful oil company doctors and it paid little attention to university interests apart from the kudos and authority it could claim by virtue of its university association. It expected to be judged on its balance sheet and its financial contribution to the university, and this was intended to support the academic aspect of the institute.

The academic part of the original institute remained in the Department of Surgery. It was soon referred to as the institute to distinguish it from OMS, which further underlined the creation of separate units. Professor Smith was once again the director of that part but again his extensive area of responsibilities left him little time to devote to its direction and development. I took over that responsibility by default though I was frustrated by lack of authority. This part of the organisation developed the training courses that the industry required and carried out research to answer the practical problems which arose for those who live and work in remote places with hazardous environments. It also attempted to direct its research in support of the local community where possible in addition to the oil industry. It thus provided an excellent advertising front for the commercial activities of OMS.

The institute had always provided the management and specialist co-ordination of the very serious diving cases. This did not, however, attract fees, for the administrative and financial arrangements for routine and emergency top-side and diving medicine were firmly held by OMS for university staff. The institute also initially organised the volunteer specialist support which may be needed in the management of a major incident such as an explosion or a blow-out. After some time we led a negotiation with the oil companies to establish this service on a proper professional footing. After much discussion this was agreed, the oil companies accepted responsibility for the service and the volunteer group was disbanded. The new group were provided with special clothing, communications (pagers were now available), training, medico-legal cover and they were even paid provided, of course, they were not full time employees of the university or the national health service. The large contract for this service was made with OMS again however, and the service was based in the Accident and Emergency Department of Aberdeen Royal Infirmary under the management of Mr Alasdair Mathieson.

Medical service was, however, proceeding well now and research had been established in the diving area. The research needed was over a much broader area, however, and work was now promoted in an area which was of importance to both the industry and the community, namely hypothermia. While most of the Department of Surgery's current experience and knowledge was in the area of surgical hypothermia as an aid to cardiac and neuro-surgery, the cold was a different problem altogether. It was also hoped that the opportunity of involvement in support of the North Sea industry would result in lasting benefits for the communities of the North East. While urban hypothermia was not uncommon in winter the growing recreational tourist industry in the hills was producing increasing episodes of accidental hypothermia every winter and immersion hypothermia was responsible for considerable fatalities in the fishing industry.

When OMS was established it was agreed that it would support the institute to the extent of ten thousand pounds per annum minimum, and that this would increase as OMS came into profit. The ten thousand did come for a few years but it never increased. The university did, however, make a contribution to the institute in the form of a lectureship and I was left to find a suitable incumbent. The problem was that there was no-one with much expertise in this new subject. I went to see my old boss Otto Edholm, Director of the MRC Division of Human Physiology based at Hampstead. Professor Edholm had supervised my Antarctic work but was now in the process of retiring and all his people had unfortunately been dissipated far and wide. His unit contained a quite outstanding set of environmental chambers – the only ones in the civilian sector of the country. If I could have acquired them and added them to our proposed hyperbaric facility we would have had in Aberdeen an environmental research facility second to none in the world. Sadly, it was not to be because when the director of an MRC unit retires his unit is taken to pieces. The bulldozers were then in the process of destroying this fabulous facility – and no-one cared!

During that visit I contacted Colonel Jim Adam, who had been the army liaison officer to Edholm's unit when I was part of it and had helped me with the construction of my MD thesis. He had just retired from the army and I persuaded him to accept the lectureship. With the ten thousand from OMS I was able to take on a research fellow from Chelsea College called Iain Light. He came from Professor Rainer Goldsmith's physiology department and was keen to achieve a PhD. Professor Goldsmith had been on Sir Vivian Fuchs's trans-Antarctic expedition and was a keen cold weather researcher, which was the area Iain wished to study.

Proper research activity could now begin in the institute. I was responsible for a group of PhD students, who were largely involved in aspects of the care of critically ill surgical patients as a basis for the emerging speciality of intensive care. John Smith, my surgical research fellow, virtually took over the research on shock and was doing a great job. This included work on surgical hypothermia but this was now deviated towards accidental hypothermia. This aspect was taken on by a bright young man called Charles Auld who was aiming to become an intensive care specialist at that time. He eventually became a well known surgeon. Iain Light slotted nicely into basic research with him on accidental hypothermia. That neatly crossed the boundary between the two disciplines of surgery and environmental medicine and produced some very fascinating and important results. The research base of the institute was thus now established and active. Mike Childs was still pursuing his quest for the cause of episodes of unconsciousness at depth in divers so it was also broad based.

The other element of the new medical system was of course training, which is where the appointment of Colonel Adam was important. He was a very good teacher and administrator, and he proceeded to elaborate an excellent first aid course from his military experience, which was refined as experience of the offshore environment was acquired. That course is the basic course taught to this day in remote health care and the institute was fortunate to recruit James Adam to its banner. The course became popular as the industry recognised its importance and the colonel agreed to hold it every week. Fees were charged for these courses and training eventually became the main source of funding for the institute.

When it became necessary to expand the training staff advice was sought from Mr Ian Johnson, the senior nurse tutor at Foresterhill College, who was considered to be one of the best nurse teachers in the business. After recommending Bill Morgan, who quickly left to join Shell, Ian put himself forward. He was a hard worker and he established a very fine training division for the institute which became famous both at home and abroad. When John Brebner also joined a year later it was necessary to keep clear of the principal of Foresterhill College for some time!

The basic course was designed to allow for the management by laymen of seriously injured or ill personnel who may have to be cared for during a considerable time interval if the weather was bad or they were located in a remote place. Communication with a doctor was thus important but was an initial problem since communication technology was then rudimentary. The trainees were taught to communicate what a doctor needed to know to determine what advice to give. Equally, the doctor had to be taught how to provide advice. To do that effectively he needed to have some idea of the state of knowledge of the offshore personnel and what equipment they had at their disposal. Thus medical training was just as important as the training of remotely based laymen. These concepts seem obvious today but were all new at that time and had to be articulated and established. There gradually emerged a need for many other special courses in areas such as diving medicine and environmental health, but the central basic first aid course was special since it was designed for remote industrial workers who had to cope with often severe environmental hazards and difficult communications.

A new type of health worker began to appear on the offshore installations called a rig medic, who were recruited by companies to provide first-line medical support offshore. They had not been found in the civilian sector before but were common in the services where they were known as sick berth attendants. They were soon supplemented by registered nurses. The military medics fared better initially since they were used to functioning on their own initiative. The state registered nurses had a greater range of theoretical training but they were used to acting in response to medical directions. Both groups, however, needed much further training for they were faced with conditions which were often new to them, such as environmental medicine, diving medicine, dental emergencies etc. The training needs were identified and appropriate new courses were developed, validated and introduced. This was quite complex and needed advice and involvement from a variety of specialists.

The training courses were fully subscribed and well received by both the industry and the personnel themselves, who were largely enthusiasts and keen to learn. The teachers were also enthusiastic and there was never difficulty in gaining support from the consultants of Grampian who were a most excellent group. When the Piper Alpha rig blew up in 1986, there was an effective specialist team system in operation which immediately went into action, as did the well rehearsed and effective hospital disaster plan, which fitted in well with the major civil disaster plan organised by the Grampian Police force and the oil companies. The offshore work force was well trained by that time – both the rig medics and their first aid assistant casualty handling teams. In fact when the specialists and first line doctors arrived offshore the rig medics with their first aid assistants had carried out most of the initial care required, so that all the doctors had to do was supervise the evacuation of the casualties. At the subsequent enquiry there were many criticisms and recommendations made of the industry but it was gratifying that there was no criticism of the medical response. There is little doubt, however, that the situation would have been very different if the disaster had taken place ten years earlier.

There was now an effective training and an effective research division that provided access to a funding stream which allowed the recruitment of the increased staff needed. The institute had become a power in the land, we were well known and representatives were invited to attend many conferences and to join a variety of committees. Medical advice was mainly sought in the special areas of diving and hypothermia. Diving accidents were still common and hypothermia in the hills was reported in the press practically every week during winter. Every time there was a serious incident I was asked to comment for the press, local radio or to appear on Grampian television, so the institute became something of a local legend in Aberdeen.

The institute was still part of the Department of Surgery, however, a rather clumsy arrangement that was beginning to cramp the style of both surgery and environmental medicine. During this developing phase much travel was needed if the institute was to be able to maintain its position of leadership in offshore and environmental medicine. The Department of Surgery was a very busy and committed department; Professor George Smith had many important duties in the nation as well as being ultimately responsible for the teaching of both undergraduate and post-graduate surgery and the direction of the medical faculty as dean. Equally, both Professor Smith and I were consultant surgeons with a full clinical and teaching load. I had taken on the management and direction of the academic aspects of the institute but was becoming concerned about the time I had to spend on institute affairs both within and outside Aberdeen in view of my surgical responsibilities. I felt that a consultant surgeon needed to be available if I carried out major surgical procedures. I always taught that a successful, major, surgical procedure required detailed attention to three areas from the surgeon – pre-operative preparation, the operation itself and post-operative management. Each phase was equally important and required time.

There had been discussion behind the scenes for a while and eventually the vice-chancellor, Sir Fraser Noble, called a meeting where he stated that the institute was now a big and expanding project which clearly required a full time director and independent status in the university. The result of the deliberations was duly announced by the vice-chancellor who concluded that the institute should be: "Delivered from the Department of Surgery by caesarean section." Not everyone was pleased about this but it was a timely decision and allowed the institute to develop without constraints at a pace related to the resources available to it. There was a further discussion about the appointment of the full time director. Some felt that the post should have been advertised, but it wasn't clear who could have applied for it if it was. I was invited to become the director and I accepted. It really did not mean that I had anything different to do than I had been doing for years but it did provide more freedom of action. The institute was now to be an independent, self funding academic unit within the faculty of medicine.

The new independent institute was housed in a porta-cabin beside the pressure chamber and was given start up funding of ten thousand pounds. The funds were, however, purloined by the Department of Surgery in recompense for the environmental equipment which had been bought from its funds. The institute now had to provide funds for all its activities and could no longer have access to facilities by virtue of association with an existing fully funded university department. Equally, I was informed that I had ceased to have any involvement in the clinical surgical professorial wards in the infirmary. The Health Board, however, appointed me as an honorary consultant in environmental medicine and gave me a bed in which to treat a diver if required. So began my second career.

A second porta-cabin was soon acquired to abut on the existing structure and there was access to the space associated with the hyperbaric chamber that the institute seemed to have acquired by default. These facilities were not sufficient to accommodate the expanding staff or projects. More specially it was not sufficient to provide space for teaching and training which was now the mainstay of funding. For a while it was possible to use the magnificent premises of the Medico-Chirurgical Society, but I felt uncomfortable about this in case the fine furnishings were damaged during some of the rather rough and tumble practical sessions of the courses. It allowed the institute to continue its important training function without interruption, however, and we shall always be grateful to the council of the society for their support and understanding.

Shortly after this time Matt Linning retired from his post in BP and also thus from the chair of OMS. He had always been friendly with me and I regarded him very highly. He came to see me in the portacabin and we had a long talk on the progress of the institute. Matt showed much interest in this and was conscious of the limitation to progress from resource scarcity and particularly from accommodation. Gaelic Healthguard had been wound up by this point, leaving the west-end premises at 9 Rubislaw Terrace which had been occupied by Admiral Miles vacant. Matt managed to persuade General Accident into providing it for us at a tiny rent, and so the institute moved into a new and prestigious building. This constituted a major advance since there was now space to teach and ample accommodation for the staff, administration and research. It also provided a locus consistent with an expanding and successful organisation. In addition the institute also retained the old hyperbaric unit and its associated labs on the Foresterhill site as its research base.

The horizon now seemed bright and the future hopeful, particularly as Matt Linning agreed to become a consultant adviser to the institute to help me through the difficult transition from a pure academic to an academic businessman. The only sad thing was that the relationship between OMS and the institute was poor and the gap widening as time passed. The institute doctors had little time for OMS and that feeling was reciprocated by OMS. It was annoyed with Matt for transferring allegiance from the board to the new and upstart institute. This view mainly emanated from the oil company directors, many of whom had suffered from Matt's direct and critical treatment of them when he was boss of BP. He was, however, of great value to the institute and a fearless and outspoken negotiator on our behalf.

CHAPTER 7

WIDENING HORIZONS

DONALD HADLEY, ONE OF THE FINAL YEAR STUDENTS, CAME TO SEE me one day because he rather fancied joining the British Antarctic Survey (BAS) and wanted advice. This was duly provided and I suggested that if accepted by the survey he should indicate that the institute could provide him with the necessary pre-expedition medical training and set him up with a research project. If research was provided by the medical faculty he could remain in his home town while in the UK. His family and fiancee lived in Aberdeen and that suited him. The survey agreed and the arrangement worked well.

Since Donald had undergone his pre-expedition medical training in the institute he tended to contact me for medical advice when he was in the Antarctic rather than through the usual method of communicating with the senior medical officer in Port Stanley, Falklands. He was provided with high quality advice because the institute had the whole consultant corps of Aberdeen behind it, and they were delighted to provide such medical advice as was requested.

Bill Sloman was the Secretary of BAS who had recruited me twenty years before from the Royal Army Medical Core. He got in touch when next he was giving a recruiting lecture at the university and was invited to the Norman home for a meal. From then on he dined with us every time he came to Aberdeen until he retired. The subject of Otto Edholm's imminent retirement was discussed during one of these evenings and the possibility of me succeeding him arose. Aberdeen was very far from the survey's headquarters in Cambridge but no-one at Addenbrookes hospital in Cambridge was interested then. The experience with Donald had worked well and there was also some advantage in the medical officers being able to achieve pre-expedition medical training as well as research supervision in the same place. Equally, there were not many medical academics who had Antarctic experience and the facilities to take on the supervision of the medical officers.

It was arranged for me to attend the external scientific committee of BAS, where I first met Dick Laws, the director. He told me that the survey was really desperate for doctors and would not be able to function unless something could be done about it. I said that a university campus with a medical school was a good place to be situated since the medical students were so available. It would also allow good preparation for the doctors and supervision for research. Dick Laws was quite impressed with this approach and at the next meeting of the external advisory committee Otto Edholm announced his retiral, suggesting that they should consider appointing me as his successor. It must have been discussed before because it all happened without much more ado. This did not cut much ice back in Aberdeen, either in the university or in the oil companies, but I had a strong feeling that it was very important – though I found it difficult to explain why. Probably the reason for the lack of enthusiasm in Aberdeen was that BAS as an academic unit was also strapped for funds and there was virtually no money available to support this new initiative. We were, however, widening our horizons.

Recruitment of medical officers was difficult at first and initially it was only Aberdeen graduates. Of these Iain Levack and Bill Freeland were early recruits and were probably leant on a bit by Colonel Adam and I. They did very well, however, and the support provided in training them for isolated practice from the consultants in Aberdeen was outstanding and enthusiastic. All this helped to build up confidence that this was a worthwhile activity upon which to base a career in medicine and gradually the number applying increased. It was several years, however, before there was a choice of applicants. It certainly increased my work-load considerably, because I had to devise research projects and supervise them all.

The basic scientific work on the cold environment expanded from the operating theatre to the urban scene, the Scottish mountains, the North Sea industry and finally to divers. All these situations were associated with differing physiologies – some very different. This work was contributed to by the BAS medical officers who became involved during their training time for Antarctic service, and especially when they returned to write up the results of their research and prepare for their future careers. During the write-up time for the doctors' research project (a year was allowed) it had been suggested that they could re-establish themselves in standard medicine and make such contacts as would help to establish their feet on the early steps of their chosen career ladder. This worked well in practice and virtually all were placed on the training ladder of a major medical specialty, in which a majority have climbed to achieve positions of considerable importance.

While the BAS doctors ended up in a variety of medical specialities, it was not expected that occupational medicine – and particularly that associated with the oil and gas industry – would have attracted so many. Several of the research projects which these medical officers took up were suggested by the emerging problems of the offshore industry. The involvement which they had in these projects did much to broaden their horizons and resulted in well rounded doctors, prepared for their future careers. Indeed they were occasionally given time off from their writing phase to take part in some of the institute's other international activities. Thus, Alistair Fraser spent time providing medical cover for an installation offshore in Madagascar, Bill Freeland helped with the care of the victims of an oil blow-out in the far east and Roderick Duncan joined Ian Johnson in delivering courses up and down the interior of Oman. Equally, some of the Aberdeen contingent were able to get a little Antarctic experience and Ross McLean acted as medical officer on the expedition ships from time to time.

Diving was now taking place routinely at Signy Island, the BAS biological station, and we were able to take on the care of the Antarctic divers and the training of their medical support. Steve Bridgman, the BAS doctor at Signy, conducted research which not only contributed to the safety of Antarctic divers but also to those in the North Sea. The oil industry was also interested in determining how to safeguard rig workers from cold in the far North. They had routinely decreed that all who travelled offshore should wear a survival suit in case of the helicopter ditching, and these had to be designed and tested. These opportunities were all easily seen but to take advantage of them needed more facilities – but as usual there was little money. Iain Light and I acquired a great offshore deep freeze and built it into an environmental chamber alongside the pressure chamber at Foresterhill. This chamber was capable of achieving temperatures ranging from minus forty to plus forty degrees centigrade. It was nothing like the MRC chamber at Hampstead or the Farnborough facility but it allowed the researchers to work out the relationship between cold and the loss of judgement and competence. It also allowed us to test offshore/Antarctic clothing assemblies and survival equipment, and even to test a heated chair designed (by Professor Iain Ledingham from Glasgow and his father) to keep geriatric subjects warm in winter for a penny an hour's worth of electricity.

We needed cold water for immersion hypothermia studies. Initially we hired a rubbish skip from the local council and filled it with ice cold water. We subsequently found that in winter and spring there was a bay on the river Dee beside the Robert Gordon Institute of Technology (RGIT) boathouse which kept a pretty constant temperature of four degrees centigrade when it was mixed with ice flows swirling down from further up. This worked well but I was in trouble when the re-warming bath in the boat house failed to function one day and one of BPs senior medical officers nearly entered a slightly dangerous phase of immersion hypothermia! I was chastened but not too concerned because I had seen Dick Laws's favourite photograph of himself returning from his mid-day swim in the Antarctic (at Signy Island) and hoisting himself on to the island with the aid of an ice axe thrust into the surrounding ice.

A retired Church of Scotland minister, Rev Stanley Pritchard, next appeared on the scene. He ran a charity called Action for Disaster which raised money so that it could provide immediate financial assistance in the event of a disaster. The charity had made its mark after the gas explosion in Clarkston, Glasgow, but Stanley was mainly interested in maritime problems and was much involved in the mission to deep sea fishermen. He ran television interview programmes on Grampian television and invited George and I to take part in his programme. Thereafter he asked if there was anything his charity could put a bit of money into. I told him that we were building up research facilities to allow us to study environmental problems outside the laboratory. We had offshore installations and diving chambers available for study but a laboratory in the hills would allow us to extend our laboratory work on accidental hypothermia into the field with some safety. I suggested the top of a mountain. He thought this a good idea and agreed to think about it. A few days later he phoned to ask whether a suitable laboratory could be built for five thousand pounds.

Eric Salmon was the personnel officer of BAS who had succeeded Bill Sloman. He also now stayed with the us when he visited Aberdeen on recruiting visits to the university and to discuss progress on the medical front. Eric was very interested in food, as are many people who have spent time in the Antarctic. This may be because it is very important to be a competent cook in the Antarctic since the cook has to be given a day off every week. A Cambridge university thesis on the associated stress of life on an Antarctic base concluded that the greatest stress resulted from the day spent relieving the cook – and this was subjected to scientific proof! On an Antarctic base it is just as important to select for personality as for job skill if murder is to be avoided during the long winters. The personality qualities that may be considered appropriate are not always those which would be considered best unless one had Antarctic experience. Eric was, however, a past master at selection and also at assembling compatible teams for each base.

One night, when Eric and I were discussing the extremes of Antarctic weather while sitting at a huge log fire in Aberdeen, the discussion turned towards living quarters and shelters. He talked about a two room hut which a firm in Cambridge had designed for use on one of the remote Antarctic islands – one room a lab and the other living quarters. Two years had been spent testing it and it had stood up to the winds and weather of the Antarctic remarkably well. When asked about the cost he said he thought it was about five thousand pounds! I phoned Stanley Pritchard and he agreed to provide the funds, but the institute would have to raise the money for transport and construction itself.

The next problem was to select a mountain upon which to build the proposed laboratory. Graeme Nicol was consulted as a university colleague who was also a mountaineer of note. He told me all sorts of gruesome stories about the rivalry of the local mountain rescue teams and how the whole project would be doomed if we got on the wrong side of people. The Braemar Mountain Rescue Team was largely composed of policemen and Graeme recommended an approach to them in the first instance. I had recently met the Assistant Chief Constable of Aberdeen, John Nicol, at one of the conferences which the institute held and so wrote to him. This was followed by an invitation to come to police headquarters to discuss the project. Graeme came with me, as I felt I needed someone who knew something about the mountains and their problems. Graeme used to appear on local television when there was an accident in the hills just as often as I did when there was an accident offshore.

John Nicol was in the chair and there were quite a few others present. After Graeme and I said our piece John Nicol asked Sergeant John Duff if he had anything to say. John Duff was the leader of the Braemar Mountain Rescue Team. It soon became obvious that John had considered the matter very carefully. After skirting over a few mountains he gave it as his opinion that Morrone was best suited for the purpose, not only because it was in Braemar close to his mountain rescue station. Morrone was over three thousand feet above sea level and if you proceeded downhill in any direction you eventually arrived at a road. It was therefore safe in all weathers. On the summit there already was a police telecommunication hut and it would therefore be possible to install a telephone for the transmission of scientific information and as a further safety precaution. Moreover there was a road all the way up. It seemed quite ideal and when we asked if the police in general and the mountain rescue team in particular would collaborate with the institute on this venture they readily agreed.

The next problem was to obtain permission from the owner of the mountain, Captain Farquharson of Invercauld. Captain Tennant of Innes House, Elgin was a trustee of Action for Disaster, so I wrote to him and asked him to intercede on the institute's behalf. There followed a very good meeting when Sergeant Duff, Graeme Nicol and I met with the factor of Invercauld. Afterwards, John Duff took Graeme and I on to Morrone to look at a few sites. He was a wiry chap but superbly fit and he romped us all over the hill till we nearly collapsed – he had, of course, already decided exactly where he was going to site the hut! This was on the summit alongside the existing police communication hut.

After much negotiation it seemed that the structure would be delivered in pre-fabricated pieces to Braemar. Once again it was fortunate that John Nicol offered his help because he obtained permission for it to be offloaded on the Braemar golf course. After that it still had to be elevated to the summit of the mountain. I discussed the problem with Colin Jones, who was always very helpful and full of good ideas when there was an issue. He suggested a helicopter and thought that Bristow's might help. Moreover, since Bristow provided all the helicopters for the BP operation, he agreed to intercede on the institute's behalf. He said he would suggest that it might be a good advertising feature for the helicopter company. Mr Bristow, however, said that his company did not need advertising – but he then said he would provide a helicopter during a Saturday morning training exercise.

The difficulties were not all over because a fair bit of logistic planning was needed to co-ordinate the elevation smoothly and with safety. Fortunately, John Nicol was closely involved. He not only knew that a fire brigade needed to be in attendance when a helicopter lands but how to obtain one without paying for it. He turned up in person and took charge of the organisation, securing the safety of the landing site and directing the traffic. He must also have secured permission from the golf club. Subsequent experience of John Nicol showed that he always made a great fuss before any important event in which he was involved logistically but when the time came everything worked smoothly and without the slightest hitch.

I wondered how we were going to get the structure erected but when I visited the site I found that the Braemar mountain rescue team were already engaged in building the laboratory, without being asked. They completed the building in their spare time during the summer and made an excellent job of it.

When it was complete it might be thought that there would be no further problems, but there were still a few – some easy to resolve and others more difficult. The environmental health officer from Kincardine wrote and suggested that a shower and a flush toilet was needed. He obviously was not aware of the geography and facilities on the summit of a Scottish mountain and probably had only heard that it was a laboratory. Next came a letter from a scientist to say that a very rare algae was growing in an area close to the laboratory and he was horrified that the area was being disturbed by crowds of people, helicopters and vehicles. It had been kept a closely guarded secret for years. It appeared that he wanted the structure to be moved to another mountain. We agreed to keep clear of the algea area, but since it was so secret we never found out where it was!

It was decided to have an official opening of the laboratory and Captain Tennant agreed to determine whether a member of the Royal Family might visit it during a session at Balmoral. In the event HRH the Duke of Edinburgh agreed to an informal visit. The whole institute staff repaired to the summit of Morrone the day before to make sure that everything was in order for the Royal visit and to set out the various research demonstrations planned. Colonel Adam waxed military towards the end of the afternoon and suggested that the stones which lined the approach road should be whitewashed in true military fashion. This was the subject of an intense argument when the newly installed telephone rang imperiously. Jim Adam picked it up and said, "Chinese laundry". After a pause he held the phone out to John Nicol and said, "Buckingham Palace for Mr Nicol". Poor John took the phone in a state of great embarrassment. Mercifully it was not the Duke!

When the day of the visit dawned the weather was once again excellent and the Duke drove himself up the mountain – twice as fast as anyone had ever done it before. He was very interested in the work and there were five research stations for him to visit. He must have been well briefed because at each station he ended up by asking a hard question and I often had to bail the boys out.

Work started as soon as the laboratory was opened. Iain Light was finishing off his PhD, which included some work on Morrone testing sleeping and survival bags. For this he had to recruit subjects for his tests. One of these was a student from St Thomas hospital in London who had come to the institute for his elective period of study. Iain met him from the sleeper, rushed him straight up Morrone, stuck a thermometer up his bottom and installed him in a survival bag in a snowdrift. It was the last elective student we had from St Thomas! We were able to show, however, that a plastic bag costing nine pence offered as much thermal protection as a fancy prototype survival bag costing forty pounds.

The whole Morrone project was a remarkable community achievement since it attracted help from such a wide variety of people and institutions – the charities, mainly Action for Disaster and Tenovus, the landlords, Captain Farquharson of Invercauld and Captain Tennant of Moray, the police from constables to assistant chief-constable, the mountain rescue teams, BP, Bristow's helicopters, the British Antarctic Survey, the University of Aberdeen and RGIT. And all for five thousand pounds!

Shortly afterwards John Nicol retired from the Grampian Police Force and joined the institute on the same basis as Matt Linning for a token consultancy fee He was a wise counsellor and his advice was invaluable in several awkward situations involving the increasingly difficult local politics. The institute was thus becoming a general Aberdeen community and academic project – of which there are many examples in the history of Aberdeen.

CHAPTER 8

TRAINING IN THE MIDDLE EAST

A WHOLE MENU OF COURSES WAS DEVELOPED BY THE TRAINING DIVI-sion of the institute but the main courses which were offered frequently and regularly were the basic first aid course and the courses for rig medics. Since this was all new ground it was as much of a learning curve for the institute as for anyone, and the Health and Safety group were not involved at that time – indeed it was the institute courses that they adopted initially when they did become involved. We had adopted the habit from the outset of holding a conference at least once per year on aspects of offshore and remote health care. This allowed discussion of what was required and helped to build up relevant training material. It also began to develop the concept of the institute as an academic and professional home for those interested in offshore and remote health care.

The new courses developed were the diving medical courses referred to before as well as courses in environmental health and hygiene. The Antarctic doctors were all granted the university status of research assistant and were thus able to enrol for higher degrees such as MD or PhD, so the teaching covered all levels.

The training department and the trainees increased in numbers rapidly, and though the new building at Rubislaw Terrace was very fine it was difficult to accommodate the considerable numbers attending the basic courses and the diversity of the new courses. Equally, an increasing amount of practical work was required as the course was modified with experience and feedback from the industry. One day Ian Johnson said that there was an old property at Kepplestone that belonged to the Aberdeen College of Education and which was now surplus to its requirements. He had spoken to the college and found they would be happy to let us use the bottom flat for training – and for a tiny token rent! This was ideal for the training department, allowed for considerable expansion, was perfect for practical sessions and had extensive grounds for outside training exercises and plenty of parking. This really made it possible to develop the training work. We could even provide for catering since there were kitchens. The training department thus moved over which in turn allowed enlargement of the research department, providing accommodation for the increasing number of Antarctic doctors who were either preparing to go south or were writing up their research on return. It also allowed space to accommodate elective students from other universities, and attachments on sabbaticals from both Aberdeen and other universities.

The institute was self financing and the mainstay of funding was certainly teaching, so the Kepplestone development was very important. We had an increasing number of research grants, but there was little profit to be made from them since the university already creamed off forty percent for their administration. Any contracts made were held by OMS, such as those for the diving transfer capsules and the re-organisation of the specialist team contract with the industry. The institute had growing overheads and administrative costs, which all had to be bourne from training. The other lucrative area was, of course, the practice of offshore medicine, with its routine and emergency advisory services and specifically its medical examinations for fitness to work. This funding was denied to the institute and funds raised from institute personnel who provided such services were retained by OMS.

We thus sought other ways of increasing our income consistent with our interests and terms of reference. The courses were of a very high standard and taught by very good teachers. They were thus popular and attended by many overseas personnel, for they were new and not available elsewhere. After one of these courses Tony Garner came to speak to me, a pleasant young doctor who worked for the Dubai Petroleum Company. He said: "You have told us all about diving in cold water and the problems associated with work in cold climates, but we have just as many problems with environmental heat. Why do you not come to the Middle East and look at these problems?" Some weeks later the arrangements were made for me to spend three days in Dubai with The Dubai Petroleum Company (DPC), followed by three days with Petroleum Development Oman and finally three days with the Qatar General Petroleum Company (Offshore). It was a memorable trip and I was pleased to note that I was travelling all the way first class on British Airways, certainly not the usual way for university academics to travel.

It was July and when the door of the aircraft was opened we were hit by a wall of hot, wet air, which I had not experienced since my first trip to Singapore. When I got off the plane I was immediately met by two young Arabs in national dress – an impressive sight. I was ushered by them through passport control and customs by the fast route and taken to meet Tony Garner, who was waiting to escort me to my residence. He said he would call for me at six thirty next morning. That was a bit of a problem because it was now two in the morning, I was exhausted after the long journey, the good food and the booze, and there was a three hour time difference which meant that he would be calling at three thirty by my internal clock. I had forgotten to bring an alarm clock so I endeavoured to stay awake in case I slept in. I had not yet become a laid back, international jet setter.

Tony duly arrived at six thirty to keep his promise to show me about heat and we took a helicopter to an oil tanker which was anchored offshore. Since it was July the temperature was between forty and fifty degrees centigrade with high offshore humidity. We then went down to the engine room where we found a couple of engineers working on the fault. There were another two engineers in a cool room and the two teams alternated in ten minute shifts. That was heat! When I described this to my marine engineer father-in-law, George Riste, he said that he knew exactly what I was talking about. He remembered going up the Gulf in summer in a coal burner!

When we got back, showered and underwent re-hydration we headed to the DPC medical clinic where we met the chief medical officer, David De Rhenzy Martin, another remarkable man. He had just completed the design and construction of his clinic. This was the first really well designed clinic in the Middle East and it became the model that everyone else wanted to copy. The only problem was that they all wanted theirs to be bigger. Having shown me around the very fine clinic David took me for a look round Dubai and a swim in the Indian Ocean, where I was amazed to find that the water was like a hot bath. Since Tony had asked me to come out to see what environmental heat was really like I invited David to come to Aberdeen in November to see what cold was like. He duly came and I took him to the Beryl Platform east of Shetland in a real winter gale. We could hardly get off the heli-deck so fierce was the wind and we spent the night in Hillswick – the furthest north guest house in Shetland. I think he was duly impressed and honour was retained in the field of environmental hostility. David had been a young district commissioner in the Sudan wandering about the desert on a camel with a local guide many years before. He got into trouble trying to help at a difficult childbirth and illness, feeling so useless that he resigned and took himself off to St Thomas's in London to study medicine. He then returned to the Middle East and practised medicine there very effectively until he retired.

I found I was expected to deliver a lecture, which I duly did at the Raschid hospital in Dubai, and to give my assessment of the medical provisions to the senior management of the company, so there was not much opportunity to do anything with spare time other than make preparations for these events. At the end of the four days there was a great party and I was bundled on to a plane for Oman. I was met on arrival by the senior medical officer, Mike Gilbert, and immediately found myself in an entirely different environment from Dubai. I was a guest of Mike and Anita Gilbert in their most beautiful house. It was on a hill, had a wide terrace and fantastic views over the sea. Oman is a beautiful place and the Omanis friendly people who make you feel very welcome in their country. At that time they did not have nearly as much oil revenue as the Gulf states, but the Sultan had used what wealth he had very wisely to build hospitals, schools and roads. He was a wise and popular ruler. His Al-Bustan hotel is the most remarkable hotel I have ever seen, made entirely of Italian marble and constructed for a meeting of the Gulf Co-operative Council. It is octagonal so that each of the seven member states could sit on one side of the octagonal table in the council chamber, with the eighth side for the secretary. Apparently the Sultan was concerned that the building would not be ready in time for the meeting so he bought the marble mine in Italy, had the production increased greatly, got the project finished on time and then sold the quarry back to the Italians.

We visited the European doctor, who was soon to retire after practising in Muscat for about forty years. This was my first visit to a traditional Arab office. He sat at a great table-like desk and when you entered you were at once aware that there were about ten other people sitting on chairs around the front of the table. When you went in his attention was immediately directed to you, you were introduced and had a few minutes chat as you sat down and ordered your coffee. Someone else then spoke and attention was directed to him and away from you. This went on until you had achieved what you came for – being interrupted from time to time by new arrivals and interjections. He was a wise man and when he retired the Sultan gave him a house in Oman and a multiple entry visa. Before there was much money around it was said that the Sultan relied a lot on his council shortly after his accession – indeed it was also said that when the Sultan needed advice he sometimes rode over on his bicycle to consult the good doctor.

Mike Gilbert took me for a tour of the interior, partly by Land-Rover and partly by the company plane. We drove through the mountain range at the coast – Jebel Actar to Niswah – and visited the small hospital there, which was very rudimentary at the time. We then proceeded to the main oil camps at Fahud in the central part of the interior and Marmul in the south. We also saw contractors camps which were very different from the oil company accommodation. There could be about twenty men in a porta-cabin meant to house a maximum of ten. The contractor manager said he had solved the problem by installing an air-conditioning unit. It was one of Mike's jobs to do something about this. I also learned that the fishermen of the Kuria Muria islands, who produced fish for Muscat, were very annoyed with the lobsters which kept getting into their nets and damaging them. They were regarded as pests. Normally they were discarded but Mike said he would be glad to take them for a few pence. This proved very popular with the Shell population of Europeans and when Mike got married he was able to provide lobster for all his guests at minimal cost. Twenty years later Omani lobster is very popular in the Middle East and presumably the fishermen are now quite wealthy.

Back then to Muscat and the presentation to management, which was entirely different since the Omani oilfields were onshore and the geography very different from Dubai. This was followed by a big party before I was loaded on to a plane, ten minutes later arriving at Doha in Qatar. I had scarcely enough time to consider what type of new place this was before being met by the entire medical staff of the clinic led by Julian Rowbotham, its senior medical officer. The first thing which happened was of course a great party! The next day we visited the clinic, various oil installations and the Qatar General Petroleum Company (onshore) on the other side of the country at Dukhan. The onshore company was managed by a BP man who had a problem with Shell years before. Shell men were not popular in that company, and even the doctors were not supposed to talk to doctors from Shell.

The offshore company was run by a Qatari named Ahmed Hassan Bilal, who was a very colourful individual. He was actually deputy general manager but he took all the decisions necessary. As far as I could see the Dutch general manager was only allowed to sit in his fancy office and read the paper. I was duly taken to see Ahmed in a very well appointed office that included in its furnishings a huge Golden Eagle, rumoured to be made of solid gold. Ahmed had apparently started in Shell as a coffee boy and gradually worked his way up to a position of great power and influence. He was a bit overpowering and as soon as I sat down his personal coffee boy rushed in and served me with Arabic coffee in a small bowl. Fortunately I remembered to take it with my right hand, to have a second cup to show my appreciation and then to shake the cup to stop the coffee coming. The left hand is of course reserved for another function.

After the inevitable lecture at the Hamad hospital I was taken to say goodbye to Ahmed and he asked me what I actually did in Aberdeen. I told him about the institute and its teaching and research function for

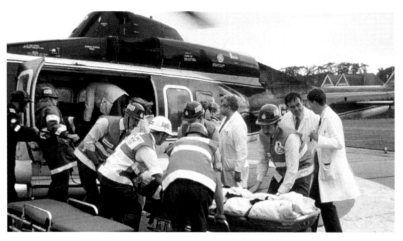

Casualty arriving at the helipad at Aberdeen Royal Infirmary.
Prof Graham Page is in attendance beside the helicopter.

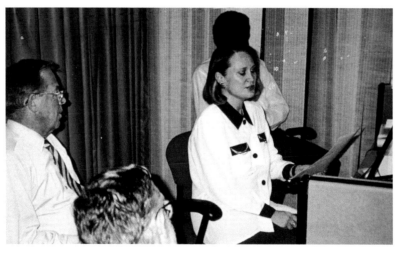

Dr Shirley Mcilvenny reading a paper at the medical school in Al-Ain to
the Royal College of General Practitioners in Aberdeen by the original
PC-based telemedicine system

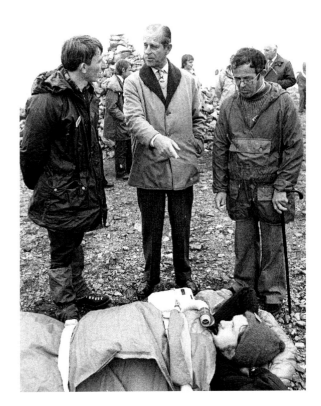

HRH the Duke of Edinburgh chatting to Iain Light during the opening of the Morrone Field Laboratory.

Testing survival equipment at Morrone.

RGIT training group set off for Cambridge in the BAS twin otter. From left to right: Ian Johnstone, Demsond Crystal, Charles Graham (HSE), John Brebner, Nelson Norman, Robin Hastings, Graham Page, William Leese.

HRH the Duke of Edinburgh chats to Matt Linning during the opening of the Morrone Field Laboratory. John Nicol is in the background and the mountain rescue team of Gordonstoun school to the right.

The titanium transfer chamber used to transfer a casualty
ashore by helicopter.

Under ice diving
at Signy Island,
Antarctica.

British Antarctic Survey training course at Girton College, before leaving for the Antarctic.

Establishment of the British Antarctic Survey Medical Unit (BASMU) at RGIT Centre for Offshore Health in 1986. From left to right: Dr David Kennedy, Professor Iain Mccallum, Dr Tom Shields, Dr Richard Laws, Vice-Admiral Sir John Rawlins, Nelson Norman, John Brebner.

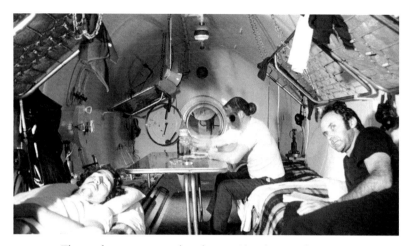

The onshore pressure chamber in Aberdeen with patient
and medical attendants.

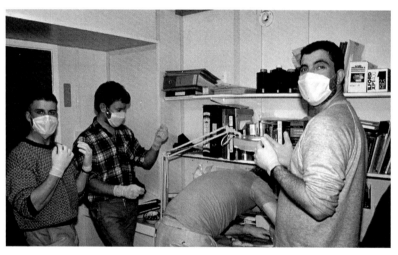

Dr Tony Maggs training base personnel in immediate care at
Halley, Antarctica.

the oil industry and he said, "You should come back and do one of your courses here".

I finally got on to the plane and returned to life in Aberdeen – 'auld claes and porridge'. The airports in the Middle East were terrible at that time. Every case was opened and examined by customs and when you wanted to leave you were greeted by a howling mob at the check in – Arabs with big paper parcels and Indians with gas stoves – while on arrival the cases were just in a heap. I soon learned the technique at the check in, however. The ticket clerk had all his attention on the chap whose case was on the scales, so when the previous case went through the technique was to get your case on the scales before anyone else did. I thought in those days how nice it was to return to the peace and order of Heathrow. It was interesting over the years to see the scene gradually change, so that now the Gulf airports are all efficiency and speed while Heathrow becomes more chaotic on every visit.

When I got back to Aberdeen I asked Ian Johnson if he would like to come to Qatar to do a couple of courses. Ian agreed and some weeks later we set out with all our kit to conduct a course. Of course there were problems at the airport. We could not get our videos or mannequins through customs so we had to start the course with very little in the way of aids. The look on the face of the customs officer when he opened the mannequin case and found a blond female in a track suit was memorable!

The lecture room was very small and stuffy, filled with a mixture of Dutchmen who thought it was a waste of time and Indians who found it difficult to understand because they could not speak English. We were not allowed to start till the course was opened by Ahmed who arrived nearly three quarters of an hour late in a top of the range Mercedes, even though it was only about a hundred yards from his office! He made a great entrance and while he spoke there was dead silence. He informed the gathered class that he had secured our services at great expense, that he expected all of them to pay close attention and keep perfect time. He ended with the phrase, "For you are all very important people to this company, but remember, no man is indispensable". In the ensuing dead silence he made a dramatic exit and we were left to get on with it. Ian coped magnificently as expected. I was not too sure of some of the material we had then because doctors are not trained to teach immediate care but we managed until the videos and mannequins eventually arrived.

So started a twenty year association with the Middle East in teaching. The United Arab Emirates followed (courtesy of then CMO, Graeme Nicol) and then Mike Gilbert set the institute up in Oman. The course eventually spread to Brunei, Greenland, Pisa and even Northern Canada. On this first visit I was treated very well and welcomed by the Middle East managers. It seemed that the institute was now regarded as the leading, international medical institution in oilfield health care in that part of the world. We had come a long way and were indeed able to offer advice which was of value.

On the second visit to Qatar Ahmed sent for me and suggested moving a team out and setting up a training business: "Go and see my agent, Munir Issa, and he will tell you how to go about it". I thought that it was a good idea, but as I climbed the backstairs of an Arab building in Doha to see a Lebanese business man I suddenly wondered what a professor in a small northern university was doing here – was I not out of my depth? Also, how would the rather stuffy administrators of the university react – some of whom had hardly been south of Stonehaven! In the event I did not go too far with Munir Issa but returned to Aberdeen and invoked the help of Matt Linning, who returned with me and helped to get something going. It was fraught with problems of visas, Egyptian interference, jealousies and finance problems, since a proper financial deal had not been made in the first instance. Nevertheless, the episode helped a lot with the finances of the Aberdeen base and got the institute established and known in the Middle East, although the institute's eventual main involvement was in Oman and Abu Dhabi rather than Qatar.

Many overseas oil company managers had been promoted to senior positions from the North Sea. They found that their jobs in the Arabian Gulf were more difficult if their people were not trained as those in the North Sea industry were to provide immediate care for the medical problems which arose. The institute was soon teaching its basic course in Qatar, Oman and Abu Dhabi. The Middle East courses were very lucrative, largely due to the efforts of Matt Linning at home and Graeme Nicol in Abu Dhabi. Graeme had now moved from the Department of

Pathology in Aberdeen to become Chief Medical Officer of the combined clinics of the Abu Dhabi oil companies. They knew that they were helping to build up an academic department which was of importance to their industry but I would not have had the brass neck to ask for the money which they advised, and I was very grateful to both of them.

It took many years for the final concept of the key priorities required to provide medical cover for a remote industrial location to emerge. They were debated in the university, with the oil company doctors and with groups such as DMAC. The distillation which finally emerged was a list of five priorities which were, in order of importance:

- immediate care training for the whole population at risk;
- increasingly sophisticated systems of communication;
- the existence of a co-ordinating group of doctors;
- the existence of specialist help and an effective evacuation system;
- on-going research and audit.

The first priority could now be effectively provided but the second had a long way to go. The introduction of tropospheric scatter and facsimile machines provided a huge advance in communications since it was then possible to communicate by telephone reasonably clearly, meaning that written requests and instructions could be exchanged without risk of misunderstanding.

While pondering this question I was invited to visit Memorial University in St John's, Newfoundland. The visit was in the midst of the historic transfer under pressure event in Aberdeen and was organised by Henry Manson, who had been an Aberdeen anaesthetist and now worked at Memorial University. Oil had been discovered in the Hibernia field off Newfoundland and Henry persuaded the authorities there that they should prepare for the medical needs before the development got underway. A conference was organised and I was invited as a keynote speaker. While there I met Max and Mary House who were hosting the conference. Max was a professor of medicine, had been chief of staff at the hospital and was taking the lead in offshore medicine. I visited Newfoundland several times after that and was most impressed with Memorial University, which had great facilities. I became a visiting

Professor in Community Medicine at Memorial after my third visit and retained the title from then on. Both Max House and Moses Morgan, the president of Memorial University, visited Aberdeen thereafter and took part in some of the institute's conferences.

The conference was highly successful and it was good that they were all keen to establish a co-ordinated approach to the impending problems. I was particularly impressed with Max House's pioneering work on communications, which was probably why he was in the forefront of preparations for offshore medicine. He had established a remote nursing degree programme in Memorial and these nurses were placed in the remote communities of Newfoundland and Labrador as the sole source of medical help. They were rather like rig medics. Every day a group of specialists in St John's sat round a table and communicated with each of these nurses in turn for a discussion of their current problems. This was voice communication only but the quality was excellent. Max was a neurologist but the only one in Newfoundland and Labrador. He had used telemetry to report on all the EEGs recorded in the province for some time and he was investigating the use of satellite technology in communications. He was currently developing slow-scan television with which a picture of the patient under discussion could be seen and the wound or whatever examined directly. I was enormously impressed with its potential in the developing field of remote medicine and was determined to introduce and develop it as soon as I returned to Aberdeen.

CHAPTER 9

A NEW BEGINNING: THE CENTRE
FOR OFFSHORE HEALTH

THE FIRST FEW YEARS OF THE 1980S WERE TIMES OF FRENETIC ACTIV-
ity in the institute, which now had very fine administrative facilities
in Rubislaw Terrace, first class teaching accommodation in Kepplestone
Mansion and amazing research facilities both at Foresterhill and in the
associated field stations. There was the hyperbaric chamber and related
laboratories, which was associated with a very adequate and functional
environmental chamber for both hot and cold climatic studies. This
was complimented by the mountain laboratory on Morrone at Braemar. For field studies we had access to offshore installations and diving
spreads in the North Sea and the Antarctic field stations, including
under ice diving research facilities at Signy Island. The latest addition
to these field facilities was the desert stations of the Abu Dhabi oil companies and we had already begun investigating the problems of working
in excessive heat. The research facilities were mind-boggling and very
full use was made of them, so the academic output in terms of theses
for higher degrees was equally impressive: John Smith achieved a PhD
and Charles Auld an MD on basic research of high quality, while Iain
Light also had his PhD (on cold environmental physiology) sustained.
Donald Hadley's PhD on remote bacteriology in the Antarctic was also
sustained as were Iain Levack and Chris Johnson's MD theses from

their Antarctic work. Even I completed my DSc thesis, so the institute certainly kept its academic end up! The teaching was also pushing back the frontiers, developing new courses and researching innovative teaching techniques such as tele-education.

Everyone was intensely busy but enjoying themselves from the success. In a very short time the dream of a self-funding academic university department had been achieved and at practically no cost to the university. It was, however, very hard work and there was no money to spare, but then that was not the prime object. If the establishment that had been recommended by Colin Jones and I initially – namely the three part organisation in which medical service, training and research worked as one – the financial result would have been much better and a profit could possibly have been made for the university. There is little doubt that the two parts (OMS and the institute) should have joined forces after establishment but there was no real interest for this from either the university or from the OMS board, although we did try for a time. David Webster moved down to Rubislaw Terrace and set up a combined administration. Unfortunately this did not work and it soon became clear that it was merely a means to determine the reason for the institute's apparent success. He lorded it over the academics and became more and more unpopular. The experiment was thus a failure and I was criticised by the university for allowing it to take place. David had, however, extracted information on the commercial value of the institute's training division and its plans and contacts for expansion overseas. I had felt that there was no reason why he should not have the information, being sufficiently naïve about business practices to recognise the signs of a take-over bid.

At this juncture the position which the institute had achieved meant that it was now consulted on a regular basis on a variety of issues. We provided a set of guidelines for the industry on environmental health for use on offshore structures, devised a scheme for the development of a mobile intensive care unit for an oil major and advised on the health hazards associated with the use of hypoxy-resin compounds by divers for the repair of the underwater parts of offshore structures (a contract provided for the Department of Chemistry).

One of the annual conferences was devoted to the problems of the various types of hypothermia – urban, immersion, mountaineering and on cold work-sites. This was supported by Action for Disaster. The discussions attracted much interest and resulted in the publication of a book entitled *Hypothermia Ashore and Afloat*, edited by Colonel Adam. This conference was attended by a wide variety of senior people including senior figures from the army and the navy. The army personnel were very impressed with the direction of the work being done and with the facilities, particularly the field station on Morrone. As a result we were asked to accept a commission from the Army Personnel Research Establishment (APRE) to undertake research in the field on physical performance in a cold climate. The pilot study, conducted on Morrone, was rapidly achieved to the satisfaction of APRE and the institute was asked to mount a major study. It had had the help and participation of the Braemar Mountain Rescue Team, the Grampian Police, Antarctic personnel and participants from many university departments and other academic institutions such as RGIT. The enthusiasm of the team put together certainly helped in the success of the enterprise.

This whole institute research initiative was thus a success story achieved in a very short time-scale. One of the lessons which could have been taken from this was the value of collaboration between an academic unit, industry and associated community groups. This happens frequently nowadays but was not common at the time. Indeed universities tended to be aloof and less interested in the industries and communities that surrounded them than they should have been. Aberdeen had always had a good rapport between town and gown, with the co-existence of the university medical school and the National Health Service on the same site responsible for a better relationship between academic and service personnel than existed in many areas. All this helped but it was not the only reason for the outstanding success of the Institute of Environmental and Offshore Medicine.

A momentous event now took place which was as devastating for the UK universities as the divorce of King Henry VIII and the subsequent dissolution of the monasteries. This was the draconian cuts in university finances brought about by Mrs Thatcher in a radical attempt to reform British universities. The Aberdeen Vice-Chancellor, Sir Fraser Noble, decided to retire to make way for the man who would need to take the tough decisions of the next decade. Sir Fraser was a very wise and competent university administrator who had been supportive of the institute, and we were sorry to see him depart.

The new Vice-Chancellor, Professor George McNicol, had an almost impossible task and one which he could not hope to emerge from with many friends. George had been Professor of Medicine at Leeds and I was in fact the first professorial signatory suggesting his appointment. I felt that a medical principal would be good and, as he was a Glasgow graduate, I thought I could work with him well. The institute was in a very strong position since it was virtually self-funding – I had almost metamorphosed from a pure academic into an academic business man. I even thought I could be of help to the university at this difficult time. I wrote to the new principal saying that I would leave him to get a grip of his difficult new situation and would tell him about the institute and its potential when he had settled in. This was a mistake. I began to have more and more political problems, the basis of which seemed to emanate from OMS. There had been strange rumblings behind the scenes and statements from the detractors of the institute about 'wheels within wheels' for some time, but our staff were not on the main campus and too busy to pay much attention. One day, however, Ian came to me saying that it was a pity we no longer had access to Kepplestone Mansion and that we would have to cancel many of our courses. I initially thought that the College of Education had decided to reclaim their space, but it transpired that David Webster had spoken to the university man responsible for accommodation and persuaded him that it was totally inappropriate for our purposes so the lease should be terminated. No-one told me. I was very angry and told Ian to re-establish the lease immediately as training was the basis for our survival.

The new principal had of course landed in a really difficult job since the whole university would collapse about him if he did not do something about it fast. With regards to the institute he was badly advised, however, by a group who were certainly not acting in the best interests of the university. The next time I saw the principal he told me that there were departments with an international reputation that may have to shut, implying that they were much more valuable to the university than the institute. He also said that he had decided to advise the court to wind up the institute, and asked if I would transfer the training part to OMS (surprise, surprise) and take the academic aspect into the Department of Medicine. I think what hurt more than anything was the realisation that the whole devious scheme was designed to acquire the lucrative training business with no thought for the new academic structure which depended upon it. It was a pity that many good academics had apparently been taken in. I had, however, no intention of taking the institute apart and had already decided to pull up my tent poles and establish the concept on more fertile ground. It was fortuitous at that point that an offer came round of early retirement on reasonably good terms – I applied for it and was accepted right away.

After informing the institute staff that I had resigned my first move was to go to Cambridge to determine my position with the Antarctic survey. I was not sure how popular I would be there. Although I had struggled manfully to provide medical training and direction for the doctors together with research supervision, I was conscious that I had not been able to spend the time that it took to run a first class service. I was gratified, however, to find that Dick Laws was satisfied with the progress I had made and said that he hoped I would be able to continue as the BAS medical consultant. I was obviously delighted. That night at dinner Charles Swithenbank, a leading polar scientist, also said that he very much hoped that I would continue to run BAS medicine.

I was happy with this turn of events but wondered where to house Antarctic medicine. I even considered my own house or its grounds for my wife and family lived in a rambling old manse on the outskirts of Aberdeen with an acre of walled garden. What I had partly forgotten was that I now had no income and might even need to move to a more modest establishment! On more mature consideration, however, I visited Dr Peter Clarke, Principal of the Robert Gordon Institute of Technology, whom I knew quite well because he had established a Centre for Offshore Survival which was highly successful. We had met quite often at meetings and conferences. I asked if he would accommodate me on the basis that I would once again be self-financing and he readily agreed when I assured him that the university principal had asked me to prepare plans to close the institute. While I could not refuse the request of the university principal I was not prepared to give up my ambition to develop remote medicine. Dr Clarke was a first class colleague and became a good friend. He agreed to my request and gave me the Robert Gordon boathouse on the River Dee, and so the Centre for Offshore Health was born. The boathouse was very small but it had been where the survival centre had started, which augured well for it was now a large and flourishing unit.

John Brebner, a far sighted and courageous training officer, came with me and Sylvia Wilcock followed. Fortunately we only had one BAS medical officer, Gordon McRuvie, in residence at that time and we left Sylvia to look after him while John and I went off to Qatar to earn some money. Shortly before that John and I had run a training contract for the Abu Dhabi onshore training company in a desert station at a place called Asab. I had used him as a sounding board in discussions about the storm which I had felt was on the horizon. He was very intelligent and logical and we discussed the philosophy and the options in great detail. He could see the future value of the institute model as clearly as I could and I was delighted that he agreed to accompany me to RGIT. I had only one Middle East contract when we started and he thus took a considerable risk.

When one is in charge of an organisation one has a kind of power base, and one of the consequences of leaving is the loss of that power base. I had seen the phenomenon before when Matt Linning retired from BP. He had a strong power base in the oil industry but people did not pay nearly so much attention to what he had to say when he lost that base. It was particularly noticeable in those who had been close admirers in the past. In other words he could now see who his real friends were, and I found exactly the same thing. I lost some apparently close friends and maintained support from some rather unexpected quarters. There were four strong supporters who remained constant thereafter and without whom it is not certain that the concept would have survived. They were Admiral Sir John Rawlins, Dr Richard Laws, Dr Graeme Nicol and Dr William Leese. William Leese was Mobil's medical adviser and in my view undoubtedly the best doctor of the oil company advisers of the time. He was a quiet, thoughtful man and offered strong support for the institute concept from the beginning and right through its difficult times. In particular he was very loyal to me even when other relationships became fraught. When he retired he continued his association with the Centre for Offshore Health and was especially involved with the establishment of the British Antarctic Survey Medical Unit.

When we came to the morning of our first management committee meeting we had spent all our initial money and still had no new contracts. John and I were at our wits end. In desperation I decided to phone the chief medical officer of the Abu Dhabi oil companies – Dr Zuhair Abu Risheh – to see if there was any chance of some work that we could claim for the future. When I introduced myself he immediately said he was glad I had called because he was desperate to establish our course in the desert. Could we cope with a month in Abu Dhabi? Before I could tell John the phone rang again and the training supervisor of BP said he had a real emergency – he had to send a dozen trainees offshore immediately and they each needed first aid certificates. He had already phoned OMS but had been told there was a queue and he would need to wait his turn. John immediately agreed that we could do it, and so we acquired the training work for both Abu Dhabi and BP and kept it. We were also able to attend our first management committee meeting with heads held high and received the approval of the management of RGIT.

The boathouse was great for a start as a kind of bolt hole or Robert the Bruce type cave (even though there were no spiders). It clearly would not suffice for long because there was not enough space for teaching, research or indeed for the BAS activities. Kepplestone Mansion had been almost tailor-made for training with large rooms and grounds for practical exercises but it had of course been taken over by OMS. They now apparently regarded it as being very suitable for training purposes!

It now became apparent that "there is a divinity which shapes our ends rough hew them how we will", for suddenly and fortuitously there was a re-organisation of allocation of local authority property. This resulted in Kepplestone Mansion being transferred from the ownership of the College of Education to that of RGIT. I immediately went to see Peter Clarke and made the case for the Centre for Offshore Health to move in. Dr Clarke was pleased to give the mansion to his new centre for a small rent. In the past only the bottom floor was available but now we had the whole mansion. This was ideal because by the time the new BAS recruits arrived there was excellent accommodation for them.

We needed to do something about making money locally and we advertised our course. Presumably OMS now intended to carry on increasing their revenues through our training business. The new centre had, however, done a great deal for the industry, had real track record and very good relationships with the training departments of many of the companies. They therefore automatically approached us when training was needed and gradually the original training portfolio was returned. John and I had even written the accompanying text book for the course and by this time acted as advisors to the medical departments of certain oil companies, the Department of Energy and the Health and Safety Executive on offshore training. When the former senior training officer, Ian Johnson, asked if he could join the centre, even at a reduced salary, the training battle was all but won. After that all the staff of the former institute joined the new centre one by one.

Unfortunately attempts were made to prevent the centre continuing with some of its overseas training activity by one oil company medical director associated with OMS, who purported to be a friend. However, there was no alternative organisation with our expertise or connections which could provide the same quality of training. Nor did any other organisation have the devoted quality of training staff who were prepared to travel to the ends of the earth at short notice. Ian Johnson and John Brebner were soon joined by Desmond Crystal, Stuart Gauld and Robin Hastings. What a great team they made. Indeed, the Foresterhill College of Nursing had been denuded of most of its best lecturers. The new centre progressed very rapidly supported by both home and overseas training.

The Survival Centre and the Health Centre were considered to be branches of the School of Mechanical and Offshore Engineering of RGIT, under the benevolent management of the Head of School, Professor Blyth MacNaughton. Blyth provided clear and wise guidance and was always ready to help and advise. Great help, advice and interest was also provided by the centre's new senior masters. Peter Clarke and Chris Anderson, Secretary of RGIT, were true entrepreneurs who guided the business development carefully. It was a real pleasure to work with these fine men. John Brebner became assistant director of the centre and we formed a partnership which saw us through several years. It was good not to have to work in isolation and we got on well together. We also managed to retain our former contacts in the UAE and Oman, as the Chief Medical Officer of Petroleum Development Oman, Dr Derek Harvey, said he would not compromise his company's training effectiveness for political reasons. The opposition never acquired any basic training work in the Gulf.

My contacts with Memorial University in Newfoundland also came in useful at this point. We were invited to St John's to advise on the establishment of medical support for the impending oil industry, with which came the realisation that what had been learned in Aberdeen was highly regarded in Newfoundland. At about that time an oil rig which was being transported in Newfoundland waters in bad weather was lost with all aboard. This caused much concern and it was decided to set up a Royal Commission to enquire into the loss of the Ocean Ranger. I was invited to become a consultant to the Royal Commission and John Brebner was invited to be my research assistant. Thus we spent some weeks in St John's, establishing the beginning of research development in the new centre.

A project which impressed me very much in Newfoundland was the exploration for oil being conducted in the Beaufort Sea by dredging up islands and drilling through them to get over the problem of continuous Arctic Sea ice. Even more impressive was the intention to build a pipeline under the ice right round to Nova Scotia. For this a very large research station was established in Memorial University, an institute called C-core. This institute was interesting because it was externally funded and had similar problems to face as the centre had in Aberdeen. It had an external advisory committee composed of several very influential Canadians, some of whom were technical, some captains of industry and some government officials. The director indicated that this group was of enormous help in the development of his institute. Since they were very senior they did not charge for their services and indeed were delighted to be invited to be part of a university project. This sounded a good idea so I decided to recruit my own external advisory committee for the Aberdeen centre.

The medical directors of several oil companies were invited to take part; they were delighted to attend and provided excellent advice on what the industry needed in human factors research and training courses.[1] The centre now had the most useful available advice and support for the development of remote medicine. It was a great move – but the original idea came from Newfoundland. This external advisory committee met twice a year in Kepplestone Mansion. The principal and senior managers of RGIT also attended and picked up the suggestions and advice directly thus saving me considerable time and effort in making proposals.

Shortly after moving to RGIT and after former colleagues had all crossed the Rubicon we were informed that our hyperbaric laboratory and environmental chamber were no longer available to us. There was also a bit of argument about whether the main APRE contract on mountain travel should come to the Centre for Offshore Health or remain with the university. Since the university had decided to knock down the Morrone Laboratory because no-one seemed to know what to do with it there would have been difficulty in running the contract! It was all very sad, childish and totally unnecessary. It was the potential of Aberdeen to become an international centre for environmental research which was being destroyed by this internecine behaviour and not the upstart centre. It had, however, already been decided that the centre's research should become more applied as befitted the modus of RGIT. The Royal Commission work on the loss of the Ocean Ranger was a good start and had initiated the research effort.

It was now time to determine the direction which the main research effort should take. We had no equipment and no dedicated research staff. There was, however, a lack of information on the epidemiology of the conditions which occurred offshore and of those which required evacuation. Without this information it was difficult to provide the best training for offshore personnel and to give advice on improvements to the medical systems. Also, the medical directors of the oil companies

---

1 These were: Chris Roythorne of Conoco; Brian Ballantyne of British Gas and Barclay Brown of Britoil. Also invited were Dr Laws from BAS; Professor Ian McCallum, President of the Faculty of Occupational Medicine; Steve Dick, Commander Tom Shields, and Morven White, Chairman of the UK Offshore Operators Association (UKOOA) medical committee. Sir John Rawlins was invited to be the chairman.

had a good idea of events in their own companies but not of the general picture, nor of how their company was faring in relation to others. The statistics were securely guarded by the companies, presumably from concerns about litigation as well as medical confidentiality.

We suggested that we might carry out a retrospective study of the illnesses and injuries which had taken place in the offshore installations of as many companies as would collaborate, in an effort to help find solutions to the current problems. The report was to be confidential and would not identify individual companies or individuals. About ten companies operating offshore were recruited and charged something like a thousand pounds each. I put John Brebner in charge of the experiment and suggested that he should consider using the results as the basis of a PhD study. We were also able to recruit the services of Dr Malcolm Valentine, who was looking for a project to study as part of his GP training. This meant that we did not have to pay him and we arranged his accommodation in the cheapest hotels when he had to travel. He did a great job but was not impressed by the frugality of his support! We even enlisted my daughter, Sarah-Jane, who was still at school, to work on the data on Saturday mornings with a BBC computer for a great deal less than the minimum wage.

The results were interesting. We confined the study to those incidents which were sufficiently severe to warrant evacuation and we separated evacuations for injury from evacuations for illness. This was because we felt that prevention of injuries was a matter for the training and safety departments of the companies while prevention of evacuations for illness was more a matter for the medical departments and their policies. We also kept routine evacuations separate from emergency evacuations since emergency evacuations with a dedicated helicopter were very expensive. Reduction of these seemed to be a matter of training rig medics, improving communications between offshore personnel and onshore doctors and developing the principles of remote medical practice.

In the early years of the decade there were virtually no evacuations for illness and nearly all were for injuries. As the decade proceeded, however, illness gradually appeared and the prevalence of injuries declined, until at the end of the decade there were nearly as many evacuations for illness as for injury. The injuries occurred mainly in the younger age groups and after age thirty the prevalence declined. Presumably training and experience in the older men resulted in progressively less injuries.

In the area of illness the most outstanding finding was that the main cause of evacuation was toothache! This was a surprise and is largely preventable by routine dental treatment, but you cannot work safely with severe toothache. There was not a high incidence of cardiovascular problems requiring routine evacuation and this was regarded as indicating reasonable pre-employment medical screening. There was however more evacuation for cardiovascular complaints in the emergency mode but the total numbers did not summate to anything like the incidence in the general population. One thing which emerged and which presumably pleased the companies was that the incidence of evacuation in the emergency mode was quite low, in fact below ten percent.

This study was the first to indicate the basic problems met in offshore medicine. The main complaints were not the exotic problems one might have suspected but the routine problems which flesh is heir to. There was a large number of upper respiratory infections, bad backs and hand injuries but very few cases of hypothermia, industrial skin complaints, diving associated illnesses etc. The study also showed trends which helped to determine the skills and background required in offshore medical personnel, in training and safety. It also began to address some of the current problems which the industry had such as the optimum age for retirement for offshore work. Evacuation was particularly low in the older age groups and this suggested that good medical screening meant that age was not a problem if the individual was fit.

This type of practical research was followed thereafter and was a good basis for elaborating relevant training. The epidemiology was extended over the years into the prospective mode. Each company got its own confidential report but also a composite report of the whole group so that it was possible to compare individual company performance with the composite picture. One company, for example, found a very high incidence of evacuations for foreign bodies in eyes compared to the composite picture. It was then able to provide improved care and reduce expense by arranging for its medics to be trained to remove embedded foreign bodies from eyes.

The various elements of our system of remote medicine were emerging. It was interesting to note that not only was BAS benefiting from this development but the personnel of the parent centre were learning also, and the contributions were from and to both the remote oil industry and the Antarctic Survey. I was basically appointed to BAS to advise its medical officers on their research but I also organised their pre-expedition training in areas which were not in the standard medical curriculum, such as the management of dental emergencies, practical anaesthetics and analgesia, surgery in remote places, radiography, environmental health, venereal disease in South America and nursing techniques. This was all organised by the consultants of Aberdeen willingly and free of charge. It was natural that when there was a medical problem in the Antarctic for which advice was needed the boys reverted to their training centre for advice. This was quite onerous sometimes and could take much time since anything which was not surgical required me to take advice from the appropriate specialist. I developed the technique of putting one of the BAS doctors in residence in charge of medical communications with the bases. It was his job to pick up the call for help and following discussion with me to consult the appropriate specialist for advice, then to discuss it again with me before sending the advice back. This worked reasonably well, though it was not perfect because I was not always there. I was also on a learning curve in remote medicine myself and I became acutely aware of the need for good communications. It was necessary for the man at the sharp end to describe the problem precisely as the quality of the information provided would colour the quality of the advice given. This was not too much of a problem for BAS since they were all medically qualified and we had trained them, but it was an important part of our basic course for offshore personnel and other remote work-sites. It was of importance for us to remember the state of training of the remote personnel, the equipment they possessed and what they were trained to do.

Gradually the techniques of remote medicine practice became second nature and one made decisions quickly. There was a case, for example, when a routine signal from a base came in saying that one of the personnel had sustained a head injury and that the x-ray suggested a depressed fracture of the skull. I observed it, thought about it briefly and did nothing. The next day I got an irate message from HQ in Cambridge to say that one of the doctors in Port Stanley had intercepted the signal and suggested that the man must immediately be evacuated. What was I going to do about it since we were at the end of the season and the last ship needed to leave immediately? I replied that nothing should be done meantime. The next day I was entertaining a senior consultant from Glasgow, Professor Iain Ledingham, when I got another message from Cambridge to say that the ship had stayed on in case I changed my mind but was in danger of foundering if it could not leave immediately. I was now on my last chance for evacuation. That drew me up a bit and I wondered whether I had been too hasty so I asked my colleague's opinion. He immediately replied "Get him out of course", but I thought about it and tried to explain how I took my decision not to do so. The signal was from the monthly routine medical report and not an emergency signal, and the patient was not unconscious nor complaining of any associated symptoms. The doctor was not unduly concerned and the x-ray probably of pretty poor quality. He was in a warm bunk in a comfortable Antarctic hut under the care of a competent doctor. If we had evacuated him from Halley we would have had to load him on to a sledge and drag him for forty miles over rough terrain to the ship, then get him aboard where he would have been under the care of a doctor with the same experience as the doctor on the base but with much less equipment. If the ship did not get stuck in the ice he would still need to sail for several weeks through the screaming fifties and the roaring forties to Port Stanley, where there was also unlikely to be a neurosurgeon. If he did indeed have a depressed fracture of the skull, which I very much doubted, and he deteriorated, we would have talked one or other doctor through the operation with one of our neurosurgeons in Aberdeen. In that unlikely event it would be considerably better to use the doctor in the warm, stable hut in possession of all the instruments rather than the one on the unstable ship, with the same level of experience but with very few instruments.

My senior colleague agreed with my assessment, the ship sailed and the man at Halley recovered uneventfully and continued his year. Thus we were learning the technology of remote medicine, but that is why a senior man of experience is needed in the mix and why he needs to be supported by good communications.

Though the centre was now in opposition to a small part of the university and to OMS it still had the full support of the NHS consultants of Aberdeen and nearly all the university consultants in its Antarctic and training endeavours. This support was constant and unvarying. The new centre was thus making progress, developing expertise in the health care of remote communities and identifying the main problem areas as the philosophy of management of the health care of remote communities emerged.

It was not only the academic part of the operation which seceded at that time, for a group of doctors had become so discontented with the OMS management style that they also opted out and set up a company called Aberdeen Industrial Doctors (AID). These included general practitioners Ronnie Strachan, Ivan Wisely and John Mawdesley, Morven White, Graham Page and I. AID offered emergency cover in both topside and diving modes from the outset and was administered by Marilyn MacRae a former administrator of the health board. Marilyn had also been the administrator of the Institute of Environmental and Offshore Medicine and was, in fact, one of the last to jump ship. I was glad to be a founder member of this organisation since it gave me access to medical practice which I no longer had from OMS or the university. This group of doctors, which had all the elements that John Hughes wanted in his diving group, worked very well together largely because it was run by doctors and the deal was of equal shares for all if it came into profit. It did not come into profit, however, while I was associated with it but the enthusiasm of the doctors was such that they worked in both the routine and emergency modes for nothing until the business was established. The OMS cartel was thus disrupted on the medical service side also. Since the AID doctors were all very experienced and competent in oil field medical support the standard of care for offshore personnel did not deteriorate. In fact it probably improved since there was now competition.

CHAPTER 10

THE BRITISH ANTARCTIC SURVEY MEDICAL UNIT

THE HIERARCHY OF BAS HAD SHOWN CONFIDENCE IN ME TO PROVIDE for their medical support and so I was determined to improve the support given. The development of our basic course in immediate care had by this time proved to be of great benefit to the offshore industry, even to those who worked offshore in the Arabian Gulf and in the desert. I felt that it would be equally valuable to the Antarctic personnel since they often had to travel far from base and there had been some problems of casualty handling which could have been avoided or managed better. It seemed difficult to determine whether there would be time in the preparation period before sailing for much training, yet it seemed important that all should be trained before going South. Eric Salmon and Dick Laws agreed that it would be useful so Eric worked out the logistics.

The survey held an annual conference in Cambridge which all proceeding south that year were required to attend. The purpose was to acquaint all new recruits with the work of BAS, the problems of Antarctic life and with the safety policies in place. This lasted just over a week and was held in Girton College, Cambridge, during the long vacation. We were given three days at the end of the conference to run our course. Since this was for about two hundred people we took the whole staff to

Cambridge with all our equipment, much as we did for overseas training courses. We needed a large number of trainers, however, because although we could lecture to a large group the practical training groups needed to consist of no more than ten trainees if good teaching was to be provided. We did not have enough trainers for such a large group so we also used the new, and previous years, medical officers. An added bonus was that the Twin Otters used in the Antarctic had new pilots who needed training before crossing the Atlantic and so Eric arranged for these planes to come to Aberdeen to transport us to Cambridge. This was good fun and also good publicity for the new centre since we got the Press and Journal to publish a photograph of us leaving Aberdeen.

Girton College was an ideal site for the course and some of the practical work was carried out in the lovely grounds, as was done in the grounds of Kepplestone Mansion. The instruction on lifting and casualty handling usually ended up with a bit of horseplay by the young trainees and the white shirts were all well stained purple with the juice of the huge mulberry tree at the end of the afternoon. This course was a great success and we repeated it every year, so we could say that all who went to the Antarctic under the British flag had the benefit of the centre's course. The Aberdeen staff also got to know the new Antarctic personnel quite well by the time the course was complete and thus had a good rapport with them if they had problems in the south. In time the feedback was that the Antarctic personnel had much greater confidence when undertaking a polar journey since they felt that they could cope with problems which might arise. Eventually, to take account of the loss of skills with time, the medical officers were given a detailed course in first aid instruction and supplied with copious audio-visual aids so that they could run refresher courses on the ships and exercises on the bases. The trainees all became very enthusiastic though the extent to which this happened was determined by the calibre of the medical officer present. From my point of view I used to shiver at the description of the handling of casualties in the monthly reports but after a time it was most rewarding to read accounts of excellent casualty handling, complete even with minor points of finesse. We were now able to fill all four of our medical positions, but usually only just and often at the eleventh hour. However, recruiting was greatly improved.

This was interpreted as meaning that the experience had done the career prospects of the doctors no harm as had been the worry after National Service days. Indeed, those consultants who came into contact with the returning doctors often said that they were more mature than their contemporaries, thoughtful and generally a pleasure to work with.

I had always been a bit worried about medical cover when I was absent and there were times when the returning doctors were no longer about. Also, I had become more and more involved with developing the Middle East connection and was still involved in national committees such as the DMAC. Graham Page, a very good friend and an excellent doctor, had become a consultant in the Accident and Emergency Department. I had already arranged for the emergency specialist team for the support of major offshore incidents to be co-ordinated by the Accident and Emergency Department and they had now been provided with communication equipment for that purpose. I therefore asked Graham and his colleague Alasdair Mathieson if they would be prepared to extend their cover to the Antarctic if I was absent. They readily agreed and when I communicated their contact numbers to Eric Salmon we could be sure that BAS was now provided with 24-hour consultant cover. This system worked well. Indeed shortly after that one of the doctors, Alistair Fraser, was casually consulted about a small lump on the arm of a senior crew member on one of the ships at South Georgia. It was a small, innocuous looking lump but it was a bit immobile and seemed to involve a nerve. The doctor was slightly suspicious and since the ship was about to disappear into the deep Antarctic for at least six weeks he suggested that the man should opt out and return to Port Stanley for investigation. He refused point blank and invoked the support of the captain who gave his backing. At this juncture the young doctor consulted the consultant in Aberdeen – Alasdair Mathieson as it happened – and he decreed that the man should be evacuated. This was done, thus probably saving his life. In remote medicine success can only be assured if all levels of medical support are in place and readily available. This proved the point.

The Falklands war now took place, which disrupted things for a while. It was of course one of the BAS ships that alerted the British Government to the Argentinian landing and occupation of South Georgia.

The war did not affect the work of the bases much, as the ships just went down via Punta Arenas in Tierra del Fuego instead of Port Stanley. One or two of the BAS doctors were involved in Port Stanley advising the governor on medical matters. Indeed a young Aberdeen doctor, Alison Mackintosh, was working in Port Stanley. Her husband was the doctor on Rothera Station and though she was desperate to go to the Antarctic women were not allowed on British bases at that time. We managed to get her as far south as the Falkland Islands however, where she not only did a great medical job but distinguished herself by marching through a fusillade of Argentine bullets and furiously tearing a strip off the Argentine commander who had opened fire on a civilian population holed up in the cathedral. She told him exactly what she thought of him in such forceful terms that he ceased firing and the civilian population was saved. Alison was thereafter awarded a well deserved OBE.

When the dust settled after the Falklands war BAS had much improved communications since these were necessary if it was to provide the government with early information of further aggression in good time. Mrs Thatcher had sent for the senior managers of BAS and asked in great detail about the function of BAS, its value to the nation and its place in the international scientific community. Her conclusion was that she would certainly rather have an academic presence in the Antarctic than a military one and so the BAS budget was doubled and ring fenced. The most immediate difference to the medical effort was the huge improvement in communications. There were now satellite communications that eventually made it possible to dial in with a telephone. It also made a huge difference to research because the young scientists in the Antarctic could now be directly supervised and advised by their seniors in UK. This took Antarctic research a step closer to that on a university campus.

I was still not officially responsible for the conduct of clinical medicine in the Antarctic and still did this only because I was keen to be allowed to do so – and indeed felt privileged to be involved in the care of a community I felt so close to. Two medical events took place at this time which shook us all and caused everyone to take things a bit more seriously. The first was a signal which came from the deep south after the last ship had left, reporting that one of the base members was coughing up blood, losing weight and having night sweats. These are the classical signs of open pulmonary tuberculosis. I consulted Dr Joe Legge, one of Aberdeen's chest physicians, about the possibility of the existence of open pulmonary tuberculosis nowadays. He replied that recently there had been quite a spate in the fishing communities working around Iceland – but, "If you let me see the pre-employment chest film I will give you a pretty good idea whether your man is likely to have tuberculosis or not." Pleased with this response I asked BAS to send up the films only to discover that the patient had slipped through the net and there was no pre-employment chest film. This meant that the remaining Otter had to take off and run up and down South America denuding the chemist shops of anti-tuberculous drugs in case this problem developed further during the winter. Also, the patient had to be isolated and barrier nursed in case he spread tuberculosis around his base. This did not do much for his psyche. The Antarctic winter is hard enough to bear without being isolated and considered dangerous to your colleagues. In the end of the day he did not have tuberculosis but he had had a pretty miserable winter, as did the rest of the base members. The episode cost BAS a great deal of money in unnecessary drugs and transport.

The next case was a man who developed jaundice and had a very enlarged liver. I consulted the Professor of Medicine who said he did not know what the problem was but that he obviously needed to be evacuated. It was winter once again and evacuation was not possible but if it was hepatitis the whole base was at risk of infection. Once again the poor patient had to be isolated and treated with great care. He did not get worse but he did not improve either. The main worry was the spread of infection in the present base but an even greater worry was the position of the incoming personnel.

Most personnel spend two years in the Antarctic and half are relieved each year. Thus there is always half of the personnel who are experienced in Antarctic health and safety. It seemed to me that unless we could exclude hepatitis there was no way we could introduce a boat load of fresh explorers to the base in question and expose them to the remaining personnel. Equally, how were we going to evacuate the members of the infected base without causing problems on the ship or wherever it stopped? Rod Duncan, who had returned from the Antarctic the previous year and I consulted Chris Smith, our very experienced infection consultant and he confirmed our worst fears. What we needed was a diagnosis and for that we either needed the patient or a specimen of his blood. The ship sailed for Rothera and we still had no diagnosis. We had decided we could not evacuate the patient by air because it meant landing at another base and we could not risk infecting the base of another country. We eventually settled for blood but the weather made travel very difficult. Meanwhile, as the specimen was wending its weary way towards us Dick Laws was on the phone to me daily and Dr Duncan was in daily contact with Chris Smith. We had agreed that Montevideo was cut off point. If we could not resolve the problem the ship would go no further south and the years research work would be aborted. This would cost about two million pounds and would probably end by winding up the survey. Dr Smith had agreed that the precise diagnosis was not so important as was the exclusion of hepatitis. The ship was a day from Montevideo when the blood specimen arrived. It seemed to take ages in the laboratory and we were within twenty-four hours of aborting the expedition when the laboratory reported that the specimen did not contain hepatitis.

Not surprisingly, Dick Laws wanted to know what we proposed to do to avoid such events in the future. That gave me the opportunity to point out that it was surprising such disasters did not happen more often when the medical organisation was so fragmented, with personnel being responsible for organising pre-employment medicals in Cambridge or wherever, there being no medical policy, no standards of fitness and no clear medical responsibility. I thus rapidly became responsible to the survey director for medicine in addition to medical research and was invited to write a medical policy and to submit it to him. I set about this immediately and with enthusiasm.

From that time our development of Antarctic medicine for BAS and remote medicine for the offshore industry advanced in parallel. The medical policy for BAS was much the same as for the North Sea industry. The medical training objectives were the same as for offshore personnel, the standards of fitness for general Antarctic service were much the same, although the standard of fitness for those wintering were more akin to the standards for saturation divers.

BAS medical research broadened to include occupational medicine audits, environmental health and dental surveys in addition to pure physiology. As time passed and there were no more serious Antarctic medical problems which could have been foreseen and as the recruiting showed no signs of drying up the question of the formal establishment of a medical unit was raised. The Centre for Offshore Health's standing had greatly improved since the establishment of the training course and since it had taken on medical care officially. Dr Alan Milne, who had worked for the oil industry and had served as a BAS medical officer in the past, came to work in the centre and was put in charge of routine communications with BAS so that there was always an immediate response when a call came through from the bases. Graham Page and his colleagues in the Accident and Emergency Department of Aberdeen Royal Infirmary still ensured that there was always an immediate emergency response outside office hours.

I discussed the possible establishment of a BAS Medical Unit based within the Centre for Offshore Health in Aberdeen with Eric Salmon during one of his visits and he took it to the director. And so it was that in 1986 the unit was formally established, the announcement made at a meeting of the external advisory committee. It was called the British Antarctic Survey Medical Unit (BASMU) and once again the Press and Journal recorded the event for posterity by photographing it. A formal contract was arranged that gave medical responsibility to me on behalf of RGIT. This was a major step forward for the centre was now entitled the Centre for Offshore Health, incorporating the British Antarctic Survey Medical Unit. The survey could now afford to pay for the centre's services, but the centre was also now responsible for the quality of the care provided. It was no longer necessary to provide services from behind the scenes and beg for help and equipment from various quarters.

A further consequence of this change was that medical research became a recognised science subject of BAS. Before that time physiology had been largely regarded as something to keep the doctors amused, as well as a means of recruiting doctors who used to be told they may even achieve a higher degree during their time with the survey. I had struggled against this view for years but the quality of the research was now improving so much that it was being recognised as worthwhile and of scientific value. A breakthrough came when Chris Johnson's MD thesis was sustained with commendation. He had been studying hand function in the cold, since the only evidence of human adaptation to cold climates was in Arctic Inuits, whose hands still functioned at very low temperatures. There was some evidence that this may also be so in fish filleters in the North Sea. While Chris also found the hands of his trainees remained functional at progressively lower temperatures in winter he eventually determined that he could not exclude a learning effect to explain his findings.

Aside from the problems of funding research equipment for the doctors I had been finding it more and more difficult to dream up four new research projects every year, especially to then be frustrated by finding that they did not have enough time to take them to completion. This meant that we tended to end up with less than excellent research and theses even though the initial concepts were good. The doctors had no research experience and until recently supervision was difficult due to the communication problems. They all wanted a project which would entitle them to a Nobel Prize!

One doctor, Steve Krickler, was an independent spirit who was interested in microbiology. He struck up a relationship with Professor Hugh Pennington, Professor of Microbiology at Aberdeen university, who set him up with an experiment for the Antarctic. I was pleased since I was off the hook for one project and because it worked well enough to allow Steve to obtain a PhD. Another good microbiological project was mounted by Dr John Bell. Professor Pennington was delighted with the two projects because he had two intelligent technicians/research assistants who were paid for and for whom he did not require to find space.

We now gave consideration to whether it would be possible to establish research lines rather than individual projects. A project may take some years to complete but the resulting publication would include all who had contributed. This was slightly difficult to sell and it took some time before it gained universal acceptance.

Professor Josephine Arendt of the University of Surrey was next recruited. She was interested in the new science of chronobiology, which was about melatonin secretion by the pineal body in response to light.

Halley was an ideal place for these studies with its alternating seasons of three months of light and three months of darkness. James Broadway was sent to Surrey to bone up on chronobiology so there were now two very high powered research directors and two continuing lines of research, both of which were very productive. This was in addition to the work on diving, nutrition during polar travel and occupational medicine that was retained in the centre.

Since we were now an official BAS science with a budget, it was decided that we should become part of one of the BAS science units. The section chosen for us was the Division of Terrestrial and Freshwater Biology. It was headed by Dr David Walton who took a great interest in medical research from the time of his appointment. It was a great help to have a supportive voice in Cambridge. He visited regularly, saw Professors Pennington and Arendt and made sure that they had all the support they needed. The pure environmental, diving, physiological and medical research work was retained in the centre meantime. Dr Sylvia Wilcock was in charge of the day to day management of BAS research and Alan Milne of the day to day management of medicine, so the survey now had a well found and responsive system of medicine.

The centre's research work in support of the oil industry was now directed to more applied and practical problems while the more purely scientific research was that for BAS. This provided a nice balance. Both the applied and the pure research portfolios were healthy and expanding as was the training work both at home and abroad. The reputation of the centre in the international scene was better than it had ever been.

CHAPTER 11

RGIT SURVIVAL CENTRE LTD

THE CENTRE FOR OFFSHORE HEALTH WAS A BUSY AND HAPPY ORGAN-
isation and the members were a very professional, close knit and
loyal group. The team was enthusiastic, innovative and the teaching
gradually expanded into new areas. We also had a close and supportive
relationship with the RGIT hierarchy, which was now keen to become
involved in paramedical areas. I already felt that the centre should be
closer to nursing, particularly in view of our involvement with the development of rig medics and other remote health care practitioners. Rig
medics were really remote health care practitioners and we had a strong
view that properly trained and motivated nurses could act in the capacity of remote practitioners very effectively. It was also felt that hospital
nurses provided with a protocol could have a much more interesting
career if given greater involvement in patient care and our involvement
with senior nurses provided greater opportunities to propound these
views. This is all accepted nowadays but it was not regarded seriously as
recently as the 1980s.

Ann Lowis, an impressive and forceful woman, was the head nurse in
OMS. She was active in the national development of occupational health
nursing and was keen to establish a course in Aberdeen on the subject.
We had several discussions with her and eventually she accepted a post

at the centre with a view to the development of training in occupational health nursing and establishing a properly validated degree course. She established a prestigious course committee and was successful in producing an excellent course. It was fortunate that we were doing well because it was an expensive exercise! We ended up, however, with a recognised degree course in occupational health nursing to add to our portfolio. This also brought us closer to RGIT management.

When the nursing colleges were subsumed into higher education Ann Lowis and her activity were probably responsible for Aberdeen nurse education being placed within RGIT – or the Robert Gordon University (RGU) as it was by that time. It was good to know that we were able to contribute in a very tangible manner to the aims and aspirations of the new university; Ann subsequently became the first Professor of Nursing there. Subsequently I was invited to oversee the transfer of the departments of physiotherapy, radiography and occupational therapy from the Hospital Board to RGU, which provided a further contribution to the university. RGU now had a substantial portfolio of paramedical courses that formed the basis of a new faculty soon to be established within it.

The centre was now doing as well as it could within its terms of reference. It was truly self-funding but there was little financial margin – in fact the financial situation usually only just made balance at the end of the year. We had virtually all the training work available and all the overseas teaching we could cope with. Indeed, all the personnel were taking turns rushing up and down sand dunes in the Arabian desert teaching oil workers about immediate care to make ends meet. There was not much more research that could be coped with either without adding to the staff. Yet the three essential elements of medicine, training and research had still not been realised. Aside from special areas like diving medicine and Antarctic medicine we had not been able to practice medicine.

Kepplestone Mansion had been a private nursing home at one time and even had an operating suite. This was surplus to our requirements and it seemed that it would make a very fine clinic. The problem was how to set it up and operate it. Our teachers were all nurses and we had plenty of doctors, so it thus seemed worthwhile to try and solve the problem. The first move seemed to be to acquire an x-ray machine. Ronald Mahaffy, one of the private radiologists, provided us with a very old but functional x-ray machine for a couple of hundred pounds and agreed to read the x-rays if we could set up the clinic. We had all the other equipment needed to carry out medical examinations since we needed it for rig medic teaching. We did not have any patients, however, and did not immediately know how to break into this market.

We directed our attention towards our sister organisation in RGIT, the Centre for Offshore Survival. This centre had a considerable throughput of offshore personnel every week. The director was Joe Cross and the possibility of offering a medical examination at the same time as survival training was discussed with him. We already provided medical cover for the survival centre's training function and Joe allowed us to come to his training enrolment sessions to canvas for custom from those who may be in need of a statutory medical examination. A trickle began to arrive but Kepplestone Mansion was at the other side of town from the survival centre. Neither was it very convenient to carry out the medical examination while the chaps were on survival training – but it was a beginning.

A completely unrelated event took place at this time that altered our fortunes totally. This was the oil industry recession of 1986, which spelt disaster for many people. The Aberdeen business men who were often a bit toffee nosed about the brash oil industry now found that they were indeed oil related themselves. The businesses of the butchers, bakers and candlestick-makers had all expanded in response to the huge increase of the expatriate population. Lawyers, estate-agents and building societies were all doing great business. Many of the expatriates, however, now lost their jobs as the oil companies tightened their belts and the contractors downsized. Rather than wait around to terminate their mortgages properly a goodly number merely popped their house keys through the estate agent's or building society's letter boxes, pulled up their tent poles and disappeared like a mirage back to the States. This grim state of affairs was largely confined to Aberdeen and its immediate surroundings. The rest of the country was doing pretty well and few people outside the area were really aware of the extent of the problem.

From our point of view training and research work associated with the industry virtually ceased. It is often said in industry that in times of financial trouble the first things to go are training and research. This certainly proved to be so. The oil industry is international and the same problems faced the Middle East companies, so overseas training ceased just as abruptly. It was not quite so bad for OMS and AID because the companies still had to look after their personnel, but still all but the most urgent medical examinations were cancelled. The survival centre also suffered a big fall in training numbers even though a survival certificate was required before people could travel offshore. The companies limited survival training where possible by failing to recruit new staff.

Joe Cross had always been aware that his organisation was entirely dependent on the oil industry and the recession saw his worries come to pass. Over the years he had, however, been able to salt away a reserve fund against such an eventuality to see the centre over a difficult patch. The health centre, however, did not have a reserve fund. It was able to balance its books but without much in reserve. I suppose staff should have been laid off since it did not take long to reach a parlous position, but it had taken years to build up an excellent group of highly specialised and trained teachers and support staff. I still regarded the outfit as a self-funding university department rather than a business and to lay off personnel was tantamount to destroying what I had taken such pains to establish. I therefore decided to attempt to weather the storm and refused to declare redundancies. The RGU management was very supportive about this and in fact came up with a proposal designed to save the day. This was gratifying particularly since the RGU hierarchy with which the centre was so close had changed in a major sort of way. The Principal, Dr Peter Clarke, had just retired while not only the Secretary and Chief Administrator of RGU, Chris Anderson, but also the overall director of the offshore centres, Professor Blyth MacNaughton, had both died suddenly.

It was decided to amalgamate the survival centre with the health centre and to form them into a limited liability company. The survival centre was much larger than the health centre and had a reserve fund to help achieve this. This put the health group at something of a disadvantage and resulted in a change of philosophy towards pure business principles with a profit motive so that the shareholders could see a dividend. John Brebner was very keen on this approach but some of the others, including me, were less enthusiastic. I felt that the unit would lose its ability to determine its direction in developing both teaching and research work if everything needed to show an immediate profit. It seemed to convert the unit from free thinking academics to a bunch of shop-keepers! Twenty years later this is, of course, the way British universities and royal colleges are all run. The profit motive seems to govern all major decisions taken. It was, however, not the principle upon which the great British universities, colleges and seats of learning was based and which led the world in scientific discovery and innovation – and which, in its turn, formed the basis of Britain's commercial superiority in the world. There was not much alternative, however, and so RGIT Survival Centre Ltd duly emerged in 1990.

Joe Cross was managing director, I was Medical Director and there were two directors from the RGU board of governors – the Principal, David Kennedy, and an oil company executive.[1] A local school beside the survival centre was acquired and converted for use using Joe Cross's reserve fund. The new premises were quite excellent and there was loads of room for the research department. Also, the health group was reunited with the former University of Aberdeen colleagues, Iain Light and Hamish Dingwall, who had been very active in research in the survival centre. The recession did not last too long fortunately and training rapidly took off in both survival and health modes, which included overseas training. It was a very busy time since the industry had a backlog.

Most of those involved in the Centre for Offshore Health remember it with great affection even now. It was probably the happiest phase of the development of remote medicine for those involved over the years. It was now possible, however, to recruit additional staff and to offer a safe and enhanced career structure. Indeed some excellent teachers were rapidly acquired who were broad based and capable of operating effectively in the new style of organisation. This included such men as Harry Horsley, a nurse who had looked after an Antarctic base very effectively when we could not find a doctor. Unfortunately Tom Shields

---

1 Mr Alex Mair was appointed Chairman and John Cadger Finance Director. Andrew Avery managed the survival side and John Brebner the medical side.

and Sylvia Wilcock moved to another part of RGIT where they could develop their research more freely, without commercial pressure. Ann Lowis also departed to the School of Social Sciences where she rapidly developed nursing courses very effectively.

It was a pity to lose the expertise of Tom, Sylvia and Ann and it seemed to narrow involvement down to the teaching and research associated with the practice of remote medicine. The major step forward was the ability to practise medicine. The concept was of selling the pre-employment and repeat medical examinations together with the statutory survival courses. This would save the industry much time and provide the greater economy it was always keen to achieve.

The first move was to build a clinic. Since the resources were now available to do this it was not long we had a fine one. It was an almost instant success and nurses had to be hired rapidly, followed by a radiographer and more and more doctors. Mike Doig was the first full time occupational physician to be employed and he was soon able to take on a trainee occupational physician, Findlay Dick. It was a good training unit because Finlay was soon Senior Lecturer in Occupational Medicine at Aberdeen university. Emergency services were not offered initially but it was not long before they were. The association with the Accident and Emergency Department for Antarctic cover had been continued and Graham Page now became associated with the new company and was made a visiting professor. Since he was trained in diving medicine and was still involved with Tom Shields and Aberdeen Industrial Doctors it was now possible to offer an excellent diving medical service. We soon began to pick up contracts with more and more diving companies. I was still a member of DMAC and Graham Page had been invited to join. I had also become a member of the Royal Navy Personnel Research Committee. As far as the competition with OMS was concerned this was now pretty well game, set and match!

Dr Bruce Howie retired from his post as Chief Administrative Medical Officer of Grampian Area Health Board at about this time. He told me that he considered I had received a raw deal from the university and his last act was to appoint me as Honorary Consultant Physician in Environmental Medicine to Grampian Area Health Board. He also provided me with beds at the infirmary for diving and other environmental illnesses. I was now a consultant physician having made the unusual change from the consultant surgeon post I had held a few years before.

After the top-side emergency service was established we were able to afford sufficient medical manpower for me to concentrate on other areas. One such was a request to provide a full medical service for a clinic in Yemen at Sanna'a. This was for a consortium of oil companies exploring various inhospitable areas of Yemen for oil, which had only become available after the Russians had withdrawn from the country early in Perestroika. On my first visit to Sanna'a I was met by a wild tribesman at the airport in the middle of the night who took me to a hotel. On the way we were stopped several times and a Kalashnikov thrust through the window. I thought they were terrorists or bandits but apparently they were traffic policemen! When I was checking in at the airport for the return flight I noticed that the man looking after the security x-ray apparatus had gone off for a cup of tea leaving a rather gormless character in charge. A man came along and put his case on the x-ray platform. A large gun appeared on the screen. The attendant imperiously demanded that he should open the case. He did this and the attendant removed the gun and examined it carefully before returning it to the case and handing it back! When the gunman went through he opened his case and handed the gun to one of his pals. The proper attendant then returned and his deputy told him about the incident and pointed out the owner of the gun. The attendant then imperiously strode into the departures lounge and accosted the culprit who opened his case, which was now empty.

The Sanna'a contract meant staffing and equipping a main clinic, establishing communications with the remote sites, keeping the clinic supplied with drugs and arranging evacuations for serious injuries and illness. This venture was immediately successful due to securing the services of Derek Harvey, who had recently retired from Shell where he had held the posts of Senior Medical Officer in Oman and Chief Medical Officer in Brunei. The project was very similar to the British Antarctic Survey Medical Unit but on a much smaller scale. Shortly afterwards a similar clinic was set up in Aden and once again it was possible to secure the services of another of Shell's former senior medical officers, Donald McKenzie. Remote medicine was thus being practised for the oil industry but there was a long way to go before its full potential was realised elsewhere. This had to await the development of technological advances in communications.

I visited the developments in Sanna'a after we appointed Derek Harvey and when Donald McKenzie was setting up the clinic in Aden. John Cadger came along on that occasion to look at the commercial aspect of the contracts and we went from Sanna'a to Aden by road. The road was pretty rough but the countryside was very beautiful. There was considerable unrest in the country at the time, however, and it was a bit hair-raising. The Yemenis are very nice people but in the country districts there were still warlords who controlled their territories rigidly. To demonstrate their power or disapproval of the government they frequently stopped expatriates and took them hostage. They did not harm them though, and often looked after them well. Indeed one hostage got on so well with his host that he suggested that he should marry his daughter! When he said he already had a wife this did not cut much ice – he was even offered a second daughter in addition. He was in some danger, however, since he was apparently insulting not only the daughters but his host.

Aden was very rough and no maintenance had been undertaken since the British left. When it was time to leave there was serious trouble and the airport was closed. We were told that it was too dangerous to attempt the journey by road and that we should stay where we were. John was in a great rush to get back and I had a meeting in Dubai that I was keen to attend. After some thought we remembered that we were in the midst of the holy month of Ramadan. I told John that the populace would be celebrating the festival during the hours of darkness at night and would probably go to bed after dawn. If we hired a car and started our journey at dawn we might just reach Sanna'a by the time the populous got up again. This we did, and nearly made it without incident, but a few miles short of Sanna'a a crowd of tribesmen emerged and stopped the car. The ubiquitous kalashnikov was thrust through the window and the driver removed. It was not clear what happened outside but the driver was returned rather than being shot, and we were able to complete the journey and keep our meetings. It was an exciting episode.

Thus the three medical elements of the original concept; medical service, training and research were finally combined into one highly successful organisation. This indeed confirmed that if the Institute of Environmental and Offshore Medicine had been set up as Colin and I recommended, with the three medical elements working together, there is no doubt that it would rapidly have become a self funding academic unit – and may even have been in a position to provide funds for the university that could have helped to avoid some of the problems following the draconian financial cuts. It would certainly have developed into a major international unit providing medical direction not only for exotic parts of the world but for the remote areas of Scotland, which needed such systems of medicine thirty or forty years later.

We now had space to develop the three elements of remote medicine together. BASMU was fully staffed and capable of providing a first class service for the survey. Alan Milne had developed considerable expertise and knowledge in diving medicine. In addition to his duties with BAS he was responsible for developing and running diving courses, both introductory and advanced, and also for looking after diving medical problems when they occurred either in the North Sea practice or in the Antarctic. Dr Wendy Haston became overall research supervisor for the centre in addition to her responsibility for BAS research. When the survival part appointed a further senior research physiologist, Dr Sue Coleshaw, who was a very well recognised figure in thermal research, we achieved a concentration of expertise in cold environmental and hyperbaric research that was as impressive as any in the civilian sector of the nation. The board and shareholders of the new company hardly appreciated what they had achieved. They were happy with us, however, as the company was making a profit.

BASMU was certainly a unit to be proud of. When I attended a meeting of the international Antarctic science group (SCAR) in Tasmania I was pleased to find that the medical arrangements we had were better than any other nation working in the Antarctic in the world – including Australia and USA. Equally our medical research approach was very much better in organisation and delivery than anything I found in the international scene. Once again this included America, whose research was separate from medical resources even though the research director was a scientist of considerable renown. The same was true of France, which had to depend on military personnel directed reluctantly into the service. This was in spite of the fact that Dr Rivolier of Reims was the leading Antarctic medical researcher of the day.

The main training activity in health care now settled down into a routine weekly activity with as much overseas training as could be coped with. Rig medic courses were also carried out routinely and there was funding to develop new ideas such as human simulation equipment and complex emergency exercises. The teaching staff was also increased to cope with the increased numbers. They participated in survival training also to the benefit of both the survival and the medical courses. The preparatory first aid courses for BAS at Girton College also developed amazingly in popularity and importance. It was even possible to introduce guest lecturers such as from the developing Health and Safety Executive.

One area which really needed improvement was that of medical communication. This was the second priority of the system after training. Communications were poor originally, and though there had been considerable improvements they were far from perfect. The recent establishment of satellite communications was a major step forward and the clear telephone discussions now possible with the Antarctic bases were amazing.

The potential value of telemedicine in the health care of remote communities had burst upon me with great force when I saw what Max House in Newfoundland was achieving, but only slowscan television was available at first. John Brebner and I had tried to determine whether it was good enough to transmit x-ray images by sending them back and forth across the Atlantic to Newfoundland, using a senior radiologist in both places. Professor Lewis Gillanders acted in Aberdeen and got the diagnosis right each time – but only just. The conclusion was that it was really not good enough for routine use. We next transmitted some x-rays from the Antarctic to Aberdeen using the same equipment. I was in Rothera station on Christmas day, 1986, and John was in Aberdeen. We struggled for an hour or so with the technology and eventually realised that the problem was that the path from the radio cabin on RRS Bransfield to the satellite was interrupted by the ship's funnel. When the ship was moved so that the funnel was not in the way we obtained a reasonable series of images transmitted half way round the world. I was quite comfortable in the radio cabin of Bransfield in the Antarctic but John was suffering from incipient hypothermia in his office in the Aberdeen centre because the administration had closed down the heating over Christmas to save money!

I was determined to pursue the development of telemedicine with vigour since we now regarded sophisticated communications to be almost as important as training of the population at risk. The analogue equipment available originally was, however, just not good enough to provide the quality of image required. When digital equipment became available the potential changed completely. We built a telecommunication laboratory in the research department consisting of two rooms joined by wires with a camcorder in each and tried to evaluate the difference it would make for diagnosis and management. It did not take long for me to be convinced that this would constitute a major advance in the health care of those who lived and worked in remote places, but it was strangely difficult to persuade my colleagues of this. Fortunately a young doctor called Ross Mclean came to the centre to work on a project and saw its value. He turned out to be a man of great resource and inventiveness and we were able to solve many of the technical problems quite quickly. For example, if an abdominal examination was being carried out remotely by a nurse it was necessary for the camera to be placed so that the remote physician could see both the abdomen and the patient's face. It also seemed important to have a protocol which could be faxed in advance of the consultation if a certain amount of economy was to be practised in satellite time. It soon became clear that Ross Mclean was a really gifted young scientist and doctor. He ended up in a very senior position in an American pharmaceutical company. The problem was that though Ross and I were excited about this development we could not really interest our colleagues in it and so development was slow. As usual there was no money available to push it forward as fast as we wished. Neither the survival centre, the Antarctic survey nor the offshore industry could see its value.

One man who was soon convinced though was Dr Alexander McKenzie, president of the Aberdeen Medico-Chirurgical Society. He organised a visit of senior Scottish doctors from the Scottish Office and the royal colleges to the centre and they were all very impressed with the potential of the medium. People were only convinced when they actually saw a demonstration. There was still a bit to go, however, before it achieved acceptance by central agencies.

We now had access to a large variety of hostile, physical environments for study. The final and most difficult environment was next added to our portfolio: space. I was invited to join a committee of the European Space Agency as the UK man, to determine the medical provisions necessary for space exploration. This was very interesting and much of Aberdeen's developing understanding of the medical problems associated with remote places and hostile environments was indeed relevant to space. I was thus able to make quite a contribution to the discussions, although hampered by my inability to communicate easily in French. It was an English speaking committee but they all preferred to communicate in French. I noticed that when I entered the room there was a sudden silence. This was not because they had been talking about me but because they were guilty about speaking French!

The European Space Agency was planning for the medical aspects of manned space travel. This brought me into contact with many other Antarctic agencies, for I soon discovered that Dr Rivolier was a member as was his colleague, Dr Clive Bachelard. Des Lugg of the Australian Antarctic establishment (ANARE) was also associated with space medicine and was a member. It was considered that an Antarctic station was a good training station for astronauts but they were never able to have the case accepted.

We acquired several research contracts from the European Space Agency for the centre, such as how to manage dental problems in space, how to use telemedicine in space, how to manage surgical emergencies, and the construction of a data-base of medical problems occurring in a variety of remote work-sites, with a view to determining the necessary medical provision to make for long term space travel. It was all very similar to offshore and Antarctic medicine. Dental problems had been considered in detail in these situations and the arguments about the space lifeboat were the same as the hyperbaric lifeboat which had caused so much argument in the North Sea. I even suggested using the Oschner-Scherren type regime for the treatment of appendicitis, which we had used successfully in the North Sea, since they were at the stage of considering evacuation from space for appendicitis! The distance involved here was somewhat greater, however, and the cost very much greater.

The medical part of the survival centre was much smaller than the survival part, but it was amazingly active, productive and innovative, though not so lucrative it had much more potential for expansion. John Brebner and I worked closely together and put considerable effort into this. It became apparent, however, that there was a certain resistance to the ideas generated by the medical side. It was possible that there was a bit of jealousy in some sectors since success without critiscism is rarely allowed! Another possibility was the question of succession to the board because both Joe and I were approaching sixty years of age. The concern was that the succession may mean that the company would be medically dominated rather than survival dominated. It would probably have been better to separate the survival and medical parts at that point and to develop them independently with a common board, for they were really different animals, but John – and I think Joe – did not want this.

I was now clear that I wished to pursue the academic development of remote medicine and to promote what had been achieved in Aberdeen into the international scene. This should not have been difficult but I was limited in what was a commercial enterprise where the key interest and the horizons were a bit blinkered. RGIT Survival Centre Ltd was a very successful enterprise that brought considerable funding and kudos to the university but the medical problems of the North Sea were now largely solved. I now wished to pursue the concept of the health care of those who live and work in remote places with hostile environments more positively.

I kept raising the potential of remote medicine with the board. One day Alex Mair, the chairman, made the momentous statement that it seemed quite ridiculous for a new university to go into competition with a five hundred year old medical school. I agreed, and was able to discuss things with Professor Graeme Catto, Dean of the Medical Faculty at the University of Aberdeen, whom I knew of course as a colleague. He showed so much interest and understanding in what I was trying to achieve that I felt more encouraged than I had been for some time. I then met him on his own a few times and it seemed clear that we were very much on the same wave length. At last I had found a man of vision who could see the potential of what I was trying to promote.

If the full potential was to be achieved, the way forward was some form of merger between Aberdeen university medical faculty and RGIT/RGU medicine. Principal McNicol had now retired and the new Principal – Maxwell Irvine – was an enthusiastic man who felt that Aberdeen had a great future if the various parts joined together to form a major academic consortium. He had indeed already gone across town to talk to RGU. That was a major advance and the way ahead seemed clear. Unfortunately, however, the suspicions and problems which existed between the ancient and the new university were such that a medical merger at that point was not entertained.

I was rapidly coming to the conclusion, however, that the only way forward for me to develop remote medicine lay in an association with Aberdeen university where there were such like-minded people as Maxwell Irvine and Graeme Catto. Further discussions revealed that Graeme Catto was interested in setting up a remote medicine project in the Department of Medicine at the University of Aberdeen to promote the potential of the concept of remote medicine and telemedicine internationally. He sold this to the principal and I was formally interviewed by Maxwell Irvine and the senior management group of the university. An innovation which was discussed was the possibility of establishing an academic relationship between Aberdeen university and the UAE University in Al-Ain so that the remote medicine concept could be taken into the international field. I said that I needed John to work with me. The group were good enough to welcome me aboard, and the principal felt that a nurse with a PhD was such an unusual and valuable commodity in those days that he recommended John should be taken on as a senior lecturer.

CHAPTER 12

ABERDEEN UNIVERSITY AND THE UAE

THE REMOTE HEALTH CARE UNIT (THE THIRD!) WAS THUS ESTABLISHED in the Department of Medicine at Aberdeen university where it was given a room. All it had in the way of equipment was a laptop computer that John and I shared and a small initial grant. It was not much following our efforts over twenty years, which had provided a huge collection of facilities for the study and delivery of medicine to remote sites associated with environmental hazards. We established the new unit, however, with enthusiasm and maintained the international theme we had developed over the years. I had kept in touch with Sadad Sabri, who had been a research student in the Department of Surgery many years before and was now a senior man in Kuwait. He asked whether we would like to take on a course he had designed to provide his group of fourteen doctors working on quality assurance in health care with an MSc in their subject. We said it could be done.

The project was started by taking all fourteen students to Aberdeen during the long vacation in the summer when the university facilities (computer labs etc) were not occupied. They were given instruction in the basic needs of research – statistics, experimental design, questionnaire design etc. They selected a research project related to their area of work and prepared it, with help to the point of data collection (they returned to Kuwait to collect the data). They approached this with trepidation because they were not sure how their colleagues would accept their work and whether they would receive the support they needed. In the event since the projects related to their own area of work, and not an obscure problem of the north of Scotland, their colleagues were just as keen to see the results as they were and they got great support and help. As with any research project there were all sorts of problems in the early stages but these were sorted out by email, which had just become available, and they were visited once a term in Kuwait.

The next summer the group returned to Aberdeen where they analysed the results, with help, and learned about computer graphics so that they could write the dissertation during the next winter. During the following year they were examined in Kuwait by two external examiners from Scotland. They all passed and one achieved distinction. That experience showed it was possible to conduct research supervision from a distance effectively, particularly if a subject related to the country of origin was selected. Though the project went well it was clear that it would have been much better if telemedicine facilities had been available between Kuwait and Aberdeen, since the discussions between supervisor and student could have taken place almost as though they were both in the same room.

While the Kuwaitis were in Aberdeen a young occupational physician was attending a course at the university on occupational medicine. He came to see me because he worked for the oil company for which we conducted training in Abu Dhabi. His English was very poor and he was making heavy weather of the course, which was run by a professor who tended to be sarcastic. I took him under my wing, helped him a bit with the projects and introduced him to the Kuwaitis to prevent him from being too lonely. He was duly grateful and he became interested in the course that the Kuwaitis were doing. I thought little more about it and he returned home.

The next move was to establish research in telemedicine. A round of discussions was initiated on setting up a research project on teleradiology transmissions from the northern islands. In RGIT Survival Centre this possibility had been investigated with Professor Lewis Gillanders, who in addition to his post as Head of the Department of Radiology at

Aberdeen Royal Infirmary was a consultant to the northern islands. The problem was that a radiologist only visited Orkney and Shetland once every few weeks. X-rays were taken by a radiographer and sent down to Aberdeen for reporting by plane or boat. Considerable time might pass before they were reported, which in winter depended also on the weather. Equally, it was possible that the radiologist may wish another view or a repeat x-ray that would cause a further delay. The whole thing would be made so much more efficient if the x-ray could appear electronically and immediately on the desk of the radiologist in Aberdeen. During an investigation on this a surgeon in Orkney was having some difficulty during an operation in deciding whether there was a stone in the common bile duct from an operative x-ray. This was displayed to the radiologist in Aberdeen who suggested modifications to the technique. Between them they solved the problem much as though the radiologist had been in the theatre with the surgeon. This was about the time when digital transmissions had become possible and the quality of the images now reached a very high standard.

We hoped that our research project would be funded by the Scottish Office and a proposal was made with the collaboration of Professor Elizabeth Russell, who was Professor of Public Health, and Professor Lewis Ritchie, who had just been appointed Head of General Practice and Primary Care. Funding was duly obtained and I suggested that Ross McLean should be given an appointment in the university to mastermind the project. Professor Russell gave him the appointment in her department and Ross took on the challenge and completed the project very effectively. He was eventually awarded an MD for his work on telemedicine.

Telemedicine was at last beginning to catch on although it was still only when people saw a demonstration of its possibilities that they were really impressed. Graeme Catto was hosting a visit from a very prestigious medical travelling club – the Jamie the fourth club – and he asked us to put on a demonstration. This was masterminded by Ross Mclean. I did a talk and we showed a connection to the Accident and Emergency Department where a patient was examined. Lewis Ritchie had had coffee with the group then rushed to Peterhead cottage hospital. I talked about the very fine cottage hospitals in our area, of which

Peterhead is one, and said I would show a video of Peterhead. We came to the hospital and entered it going up the stairs. I stopped at a bust of the founder and told them that Lewis Ritchie was really the man involved at present – but we should let Lewis tell you about it himself. The imagery proceeded up the staircase and the video had quietly been replaced by tele-video. Lewis then spoke and after a few minutes a senior professor from the Royal College of Physicians of London said, "Wait a minute can he see us and is he talking live?" Lewis said, "Yes, and I can see the hairs on the pimple on your nose." That demonstration did more to advance the cause of telemedicine than all the writings and presentations than went before.

The training work for the desert continued into this phase and while I was there I was invited to visit the medical faculty of the UAE university to give a seminar on telemedicine. This was well attended and the audience showed much interest. I discovered that there was a committee of enthusiasts in the faculty who were keen to develop telemedicine for undergraduate teaching and remote medicine. At the end of the day they suggested that I should join the faculty to promote telemedicine in the Middle East. This was good as it provided an opportunity to pursue one of the aims already suggested to Aberdeen university – that it should promote academic liaison between the UAE medical faculty and that of Aberdeen. This was an exciting opportunity to move the remote medicine concept forward in a new area, though it had presented itself rather sooner than expected. Equally, the oil company in Abu Dhabi had recently established a Remote Areas Medical Service (RAMS), which could allow the possibility of opening up research between the oil company and the medical faculty in Al-Ain (and possibly also Aberdeen). The unit was thus as active and busy as ever. Indeed the visits to Kuwait resulted in another large project on undergraduate pre-education in medicine, which Professor Catto was able to secure, after some guidance from Sadad Sabri, for Aberdeen university.

The new unit was doing very well and I certainly could have remained there happily with that particular management structure. But one morning I had a call from Professor Iain Ledingham's secretary, Lynne, to say that I had just been offered the post of full Professor in the Department of Community Medicine at the UAE University in Al-Ain – when could

I start? Negotiations in the Middle East can be enormously protracted so I was taken by surprise. I had a discussion with Graeme Catto and it was decided that the Remote Health Care Unit in Aberdeen should carry on with John in charge and that I should go to the Middle East with a view to promoting the interests of Aberdeen university in that part of the world. Lewis Ritchie was asked to accept the Remote Health Care Unit into his department and to look after John which he was pleased to do.

Moving to the United Arab Emirates was quite complex for we had to make all sorts of arrangements about transport, paperwork and where we were going to live. I needed a residency visa, a driving license and a bank account. I also had to settle into a completely new job in the Department of Community Medicine. I knew the Middle East well by that time but residence there demanded a different approach.

The chairman of the department was Jock Anderson, formerly a professor from Guys in London, who asked me to organize the senior clerkship. This was a remarkable teaching experience for the students. They each had a research project, an individual tutor to guide them and a statistician. They had six weeks for the project. At the end they gave an oral presentation along the strict lines of that to a learned society and they handed in a written report along the lines of a paper submitted to a journal. This was real problem based learning. The students approached it with great enthusiasm and the results were impressive – many resulting in papers which were accepted into the literature. It put them ahead of many other universities and was probably one of the facets which resulted in this new faculty being accepted by the General Medical Council of Britain. The senior clerkship was of course very labour intensive for the staff but at that time there was no problem about recruiting people. The funds were available to provide the resources needed, for the Chancellor, Sheikh Nahayan bin Mubarak Al Nahyan, wanted his medical faculty to be at least equal to anything in the west.

I found this a very rewarding teaching experience and the students were hard working, polite and pleasant individuals. The girls did better academically than the boys, which was probably determined by culture. They could not move about as the boys did and thus spent all their time studying. They became a bit competitive, even a bit aggressive and often showed more masculine characteristics than the laid back males. The boys were more pleasant to teach because they were more relaxed and easier to talk to than the girls.

Dr Saleh Hussain, the young occupational physician who I helped in Aberdeen when the Kuwaitis were doing their MSc projects, came from the oil company (ADCO in Abu Dhabi) to see me shortly after I was installed at Al-Ain. He reminded me of our association in Aberdeen and asked if it would be possible for him to do an MSc by the same method as the Kuwaitis. I said I would think about it and inquire of Aberdeen. This move heralded the beginning of the academic connection between Aberdeen and Abu Dhabi and I jumped at the suggestion, since it would no doubt allow me access to research in the oil company. I had been trying to achieve this for years but had not been encouraged by the oil company before to do more than provide basic training in immediate care.

Saleh's application to become a part-time MSc student was accepted by Aberdeen. I provided supervision locally while John Brebner acted as his supervisor in Aberdeen. Some new and important aspects of research into the heat illnesses in various parts of the Emirates were carried out which was of much importance to both the local population and also the oilfield personnel. This enabled Saleh to get a real feeling for research and he moved on to a PhD after his MSc was sustained. For his PhD we studied the epidemiology of the illnesses and injuries which took place in the oilfields in the desert and offshore, and compared them with the situation we had researched in the North Sea. All this allowed Dr Saleh to have a real chance to become the chief medical officer of the oil company, which is what happened when that post next became free. This all took place while investigating the potential of international tele-education and several research seminars were held by this medium. Both theses were in fact examined with one examiner in Al-Ain and the other in Aberdeen, using our first, simple, PC based telemedicine system.

One thing leads to another and it was not long before a queue of recent graduates were knocking at my door looking for PhDs or MScs. They were all managed on a part time basis with me supervising locally and John supervising in Aberdeen. It was much harder work to supervise a UAE higher degree than a local one in Scotland. They needed help with the English, which had to be perfect if the thesis was to sit on the library shelves of Aberdeen university. It was science that was being taught, however, and not English, so it was argued that help could be given with the English style quite legitimately. Dr Hugh Ruddick-Brackon joined John at this time and between them they took a large number of theses to completion. This established a strong academic link between Aberdeen university and many areas of UAE medicine for many of these research students became senior people in the Ministry of Health thereafter.

When more sophisticated equipment was acquired our first trans-continental conference demonstration was most dramatic because we had real difficulty in getting the equipment to work. It was an educa-tional conference attended by all the medical deans in the Middle East and sponsored by the World Health Organisation. The conference was held in one of the hotels but the equipment had to be moved from the conference room to the medical school because there was a problem with the wiring. The Vice-Chancellor of Aberdeen university, Maxwell Irvine, was in attendance in Aberdeen and Sir Kenneth Calman, Chief Medical Officer of the Ministry of Health in Britan, in Al-Ain. Professor Graeme Catto in Aberdeen simultaneously taught a group of students in Aberdeen and a group of UAE students in Al-Ain on a case of renal fail-ure. It was very impressive. Thereafter the Aberdeen students described their elective projects to the UAE students and the UAE students described their community medicine projects to the Aberdonians. Even more impressive was that both groups of students spontaneously began chatting to each other totally oblivious to the very prestigious group of observers on both sides That demonstrated the value of the medium for the promotion of international understanding among students. It was clear that this could do much for the future of international collabora-tion in many spheres.

John Brebner came out to help me set up this conference (once again courtesy of the desert teaching) which was a great help. There was a growing revolution in telemedical technology and John was at the cen-tre of its evaluation. The unit in Aberdeen had developed rapidly and had acquired the most up to date equipment for testing and evaluation. After a couple of our department members left I was able to persuade the authorities to bring John out to help with the clerkships from time to time. John was a good teacher and popular with the students, but he also gained a good understanding of what we were trying to achieve. An added advantage was that he was able to see the growing number of graduate students which he was responsible for in Aberdeen. This helped greatly in the quest for the establishment of liaison between Aberdeen university and the UAE university.

A problem in under-graduate medical education in Al-Ain was that post-mortem demonstrations could not be undertaken for cultural reasons. This is an important part of teaching pathology to medical students. In Aberdeen post-mortems were transmitted from the PM room to the main lecture theatre, so it seemed worth determining whether the images could be taken a bit further to Al-Ain. In the event a fair bit of time was spent working out how to provide images of sufficiently good quality, which required the use of three ISDN telephone lines. If three telephone lines were used, however, the images were virtually of television quality.

After much practice and discussion in both centres the time eventually arrived for the first attempt to teach a class in Al-Ain from Aberdeen. It was fortunate that the chosen pathologist in Aberdeen was an excellent teacher. The students were placed in the same places for each session and the Aberdeen pathologist was sent a seating plan with their names. When Dr Brown in Aberdeen said, "We are discussing the case of a seventy year old man who had a sudden attack of chest pain and breathlessness – Ahmed what comes into your mind?" Ahmed got such a shock at this voice from thousands of miles away that he jumped about a foot from his seat. Thereafter the students were rapt with attention. It was first class teaching and it is possible that the UAE students were taught better than the Aberdeen students. Certainly the quality of the images was fantastic. Following the evaluation, carried out by Eileen Brebner, who had joined the unit in Aberdeen, Eileen wrote the experiment up and it formed the basis of her MSc thesis.

Telemedicine was thus doing well in the faculty but it was not catching on elsewhere in the UAE. I think this was because it did not have a driver and Al-Ain was so far from Abu Dhabi that I could not readily get involved. Connections were made between the ministry hospitals and Harvard and the Mayo clinic but nothing came of them at that time. It may of course have also been because of the time differences between USA and UAE, which meant that someone had to get up in the middle of the night. There was also the usual lack of understanding between the old world and the new. For example a high powered, very commercial unit in the States offered to read all the x-rays for a price by video-conferencing. They looked stupid because some of the best radiologists in the world were at the university and in the ministry!

The next move in the university was setting up communications with conferences in Europe. This started because Dr Shirley MacIllveny, an assistant professor in the family medicine department, had a paper accepted for the spring meeting of the Royal College of General Practice in Aberdeen and she could not raise the funds to attend. A video-conference was organised with John Brebner in Aberdeen and me in Al-Ain. After some practice Shirley was able to give a good presentation using the PC based system in Al-Ain. We also realised that several people could attend the conference and take part in the discussion, which had both educational and funding implications for the future. Later, using Picturetel equipment, three complex surgical problems were presented from Al-Ain to a meeting in Glasgow of the Association of Surgeons of Great Britain and Ireland. The Al-Ain consultants then discussed the cases with experts from the Glasgow meeting. It was a real success and admirably demonstrated the potential of this new medium in international medical communications.

It was now time to become involved in some research of relevance to the UAE and I looked around to determine whether there was an area to which my expertise might contribute, since I was hardly a specialist in Public Health Medicine. I became aware that the second cause of death in the UAE was road traffic accidents. This was a public health problem in which my surgical background was appropriate. Dr Abdulbari Bener, a statistician in the department, had already done some work in this area and had made contact with the police who were responsible for both the investigation of road traffic accidents and the care of the casualties. They even had their own fleet of emergency ambulances. The police were rather insular, however, and not keen to allow access to their records.

When a road traffic accident took place at that time no-one could touch the casualties until the police had recorded the evidence. Anyone trying to administer first aid was in danger in fact of being thrown into jail on a charge of murder if the casualty died! I had also been aware of this in Oman. When first aid was taught there the problem of touching the casualty was often raised by the trainees. It was usually said that the trainees were being taught for the oil companies and that there would be no problem if they confined their efforts to the oil fields. There was, however, an occasion on one of an oil company's offshore stations when a man playing tennis sustained a heart attack and had a cardiac arrest. A clinic nurse playing tennis in an adjoining court rushed over and attempted cardio-pulmonary resuscitation. This was not successful, a security guard was looking on and the nurse spent three days in jail!

It was considered possible that this sad state of affairs could be improved if the police were encouraged to develop an interest in first aid. I had several meetings with the officer in charge of road traffic in Al-Ain and eventually offered to teach traffic policemen to provide first aid as a means of reducing the mortality rate on the roads. This took several weeks and I was about to withdraw from what seemed like an impossible task when the major suddenly agreed and a start date was discussed. It was important that this went well, so we used the balance of the money from the desert training to bring Richard McLellen to help from Aberdeen.

It was emphasised that only policemen who spoke English should be sent and that a maximum of fifteen could be managed on a course. The auditorium of the magnificent officers club in Al-Ain was provided for the course. Also provided, however, were at least fifty policemen, only one of whom spoke English! I started off with slow English but got nowhere. It looked as though it was going to be a disaster until Mohammed El-Sadig, the administrator of the community medicine department, stepped in and interpreted. I spoke a sentence in English and then Sadig spoke in Arabic. It was slow and stilted but it meant that they had time to get the message. Concentration was on practical applications and at the end there was no doubt that they really knew how to stop bleeding, to look after the airway and to care for the unconscious casualty.

Not long after this, Sadig appeared one day and said that there was a class of policemen due to be taught in ten minutes at the police school. There had been no warning, which was how things were thereafter. As usual there was a huge class but we both got on with it. We became quite good at the double act until eventually Sadig was introduced to the topic and took over in Arabic. He became very interested in the subject and certainly had no trouble in coping with the questions eventually. Following a meeting of emergency services at police headquarters that the university group attended Colonel Mustapha Shahab, who was in charge of police training in Abu Dhabi, invited (or rather commanded) us to run courses for him in Abu Dhabi. He was a bit suspicious of me for a start – as a foreigner – but once again he became very interested and supportive over the years. Soon after that it was possible to request access to the records and thus initiate a retrospective study of the management of road traffic accidents in the UAE over the past decade. If training was to be initiated it seemed important to establish a base line against which to compare the effect of it.

Colonel Shahab organised an international police conference once a year and relations were greatly strengthened by arranging for a session from Aberdeen by video-conference on police training and the management of road traffic accidents by the Aberdeen police. The next year the subject was drugs and the Chief Constable of Aberdeen, Dr Ian Oliver, organised the programme from London and came out to Abu Dhabi to take part. After that the relationship with the police directorate was very close and it was possible to set up such research as was wished. Sadig and I wrote a book in Arabic to accompany the training course in the same dual style. I was proud to be an Arabic author!

When we achieved access to the police records Sadig had become so interested in the subject that he became deeply involved in the research project, and began reading around it and constructing an epidemiology project covering the past decade. The first part of the study was to be on the epidemiology of road traffic accidents in the UAE in comparison with other parts of the world, and as a base line study to allow for the measurement of the effect of such interventions as the introduction of immediate care training for traffic policemen. Since Sadig was basically an economist with a first degree from the University of Khartoum the second part was to be an evaluation of the cost to the nation of road traffic accidents. For the final year of the study this amounted to 3.8 million dirhams (1 million US Dollars). Five years later he presented an excellent thesis to the University of Abertay Dundee and it was sustained immediately.

From this work it was slowly becoming apparent that a major cause of mortality and morbidity on the roads was poor medical management of the casualties before they reached hospital. A start had been made by introducing immediate care training for the traffic police and it was suggested that this should be extended to a wider group of first responders. The first part of the problem which had initiated interest in road traffic accidents had been solved because the public was informed by the police that action would not be taken against them if they helped an accident victim before they arrived. This happened quietly but was an important step forward. The problem which remained, however, was that they had been taught to go only so far and then to await the arrival of the ambulance when the paramedics would take over. When the very fine ambulance arrived it contained excellent equipment but was driven by an old guy in a turban with no first aid knowledge whatsoever. He was only a driver and there were no paramedics or anyone trained in pre-hospital care!

I wrote paper after paper on how to sort out this problem, and indeed how to sort out the whole problem of the management of road traffic accidents including communications and appropriate command and control centres. These fell on deaf ears, possibly because there was a budget attached. It could not be done for nothing as with the first aid training and Sadig and I did have other jobs to do. The new chairman of the department, Professor Owen Lloyd, was relaxed and supportive because he felt his people were involved in an important aspect of community medicine but there were other major calls on their time also. This dragged on until eventually I got a bit annoyed at the end of a term when I was tired and I thumped the table at police headquarters, saying "Why don't you come to Aberdeen and I will show you a proper system for the management of accidents."

After that I went on holiday to Menorca and when I returned to Aberdeen there were messages all over the place saying that the Chief

Constable wanted to see me as a matter of urgency. The party from the UAE were arriving in a week. The colonels Al-Kailli and Shahab were the leaders and they had a staff officer with them. Dr Ian Oliver had organised a terrific programme. They saw the ambulance service and its training schedules, the accident and emergency department of the hospital, the arrangements for offshore disasters, the major incident plan, the police scientific training for investigating road traffic incidents, the control of speed, the coastguards, and the management of the Piper Alpha disaster and its co-ordination among the emergency services. They flew offshore in a helicopter and they saw how a helicopter could act as an ambulance. It was a most impressive event and they went off full of the joys.

It now seemed likely that the establishment of a contract to organise a whole new emergency system for Abu Dhabi with Aberdeen's help could be looked forward to with confidence. On the way home, however, they called on South Africa and gave them the contract to do what the Al-ain group said they should do! Sadig and I returned to academe and left them to get on with it. Our good friend Colonel Al-Kailli was displeased and he opted out also. It was disappointing but there were many other things to do. It was slightly mollifying when it was noted that the helicopters were old and did not really work! They provided a few paramedics but little attempt was made to train a local group as had been recommended. This did not, however, interrupt the basic training of the policemen or the research.

A great deal had been achieved in a short time in the UAE and the relationship with Aberdeen university was developing well on many fronts. The ruler departed for America at that time, however, and was impressed with American systems of medicine which he rated more highly than the British system. He suggested that they should introduce the American system to the medical school. The very good Scottish dean, Iain Ledingham, who had been largely responsible for the initial success of the medical school decided to opt out and an American, Doug Voth, taken on. Dean Voth was not in any way enamoured with the British system of medicine and he proceeded to fight with the leading Brits – who though a bit abrasive were the source of the excellence of the faculty. The problem was that he could not replace them with high calibre Americans because US professors are paid several times more than British professors and were thus not interested in relocating. Gradually the good members of the faculty moved on and the medical school declined faster than it had built up. Telemedicine was no longer fostered largely because the time differences were not suitable for working with the US. Associations with Aberdeen were stopped just at the time when a formal association was nearing completion via Graeme Catto.

I was, however, quite popular with Dean Voth. Not much research produced by the faculty was readily understood by the community though it was of high quality in scientific terms. What Sadig and I did with the police was often reported in the press and was easy to appreciate by the community. It was therefore used to fly the faculty flag. I was even asked to form a committee to discuss the place of telemedicine and its value to the UAE. I did so and wrote a good report for which I was thanked but it went quiet after that.

Despite the fact that Aberdeen was a taboo subject I was able to continue my associated activities quietly, including the pathology telemedicine teaching and the higher degree promotion. John Brebner was still able to come out from time to time and we continued our research discussions, involvement in remote medicine in the oil fields and road traffic accidents. It just meant that things slowed down a bit but it was worthwhile to maintain the connection till things improved. Once again we were in the hands of politics!

One morning, however, Morag got out of bed a bit awkwardly and dislocated her hip, which had been replaced for a second time a year before. The best orthopaedic surgeon in Al-Ain was a Swede called Dr Fleming Grand. The problem was to get her to hospital. Fortunately I was able to get in touch with the new Canadian matron of the Al-Ain hospital and she sent an ambulance with the only competent ambulance attendant available at the time. We were able to get her down the stairs and into the ambulance. When we got to hospital the dean had asked Dr Grand to look after Morag and he was waiting for us at the door. He looked after Morag very well. A short time later the hip dislocated again but it was not such a great panic that time as the logistic problems had been solved. Dr Grand explained that a very good revisionist surgeon was needed and there was not one in the UAE. The time to retire from the faculty had come. I saw the dean and was gratified to find that he was prepared to go to great lengths to have me back after the problem was sorted out at home. He was particularly impressed, as indeed I was, when he heard that HM the Queen proposed to award me the Polar Medal for my work with the British Antarctic Survey. This was surprising since the discussion was about a very British institution!

There did not seem much more I could do, however, to promote remote medicine and telemedicine in Al-Ain at that time. I felt that if I could set up a telemedicine studio somewhere in the Emirates I could provide all sorts of British courses. The royal colleges for example had many short courses on offer as did the universities. I approached the British Council which was interested but had no space. It could not be done in Al-Ain and I was too far removed from Abu Dhabi and Dubai to achieve much. It seemed that it was best to return home and try again from there.

It was just as big a problem to disengage from the Emirates as it had been to get in. We had to prove we did not owe the telephone company or the local authorities any money and that our bank account was not in the red so we could get an exit visa. Also the car had to be sold and arrangements made for furniture to be sent home. It took weeks of patient work. Just before leaving, however, Colonel Shahab sent for me to come to Abu Dhabi accompanied by Sadig and Dr Saleh Hussain. When we all arrived the colonel sat us down and told us that the Sheikh had said he must sort out the ambulance business that so many papers had been written about – right now. "What shall I do – shall I send them all to Aberdeen for you to train?" I said that was not a good idea because I was now retired, Arabic was not spoken in Aberdeen and the problems were entirely different. I suggested that Aberdeen university should be invited to conclude a contract with the Ministry of the Interior because the new principal in Aberdeen had been saying how important it was to raise money from overseas sources. If anyone wanted me to take part in the training I would be delighted to do so. The colonel thought that was a great idea and asked me to return and put it to the university. They would invite an important member of the university to come out and complete a contract with the Sheikh. That seemed a good arrangement particularly since there were more than a thousand personnel to train and very large sums of money were being discussed. I was pleased that I would be returning to the university with a considerable bounty and could now justify the emeritus professorship which Graeme Catto had recently organised for me there.

Morag and I were delivered to the airport by a university driver who duly handed us over to the emigration authorities with appropriate paperwork. We passed through and so on to the next phase of life's rich pageant.

CHAPTER 13

THE INSTITUTE OF REMOTE
HEALTH CARE

ABERDEEN UNIVERSITY HAD UNDERGONE BIG CHANGES SINCE I DEP-arted for the Middle East. There was a new Vice-Chancellor, Charles Duncan Rice, and a new leadership of the medical faculty. Graeme Catto was packing his bags to take up a new appointment as Vice Principal of London University and Steve Logan was the new Dean. Graham Page was still there but I knew virtually no-one in the administration any longer. The Brebners had built up the unit in Professor Ritchie's Department of General Practice and both developed the theme of remote medicine and telemedicine in different directions. Eileen studied the theme and associated aspects of telemedicine in depth and proceeded to write a PhD thesis on the subject. She was also interested in its applications for remote communities and was able to obtain several research contracts from the European Economic Community on the use of communications in the communities of the northern European periphery. John concentrated on building up the association with the Middle East and worked hard, in association with Hugh Ruddick-Brackon, supervising research students I recruited from the Emirates. Since this worked well John was ultimately able to recruit his own. The unit was not only entirely self financing but made considerable money for the university. They had built up an excellent telemedical laboratory, which was visited from far and wide, and they did much to establish Aberdeen as a lead-ing centre for telemedicine.

I took up residence in the remote medicine unit with the Brebners, courtesy of my emeritus professorship which I had been given before I left the UAE. The unit was running well and there was not much for me to do apart from help a bit with Middle East examinations and provide advice on the English of theses. I maintained my connections with Dr Sadig in Al-Ain also and advised him on the development of his career in road traffic accidents and road safety initiatives. I also kept in touch with Dr Saleh Hussain on Middle East oilfield medicine.

Feeling surplus to requirements and with former university and oil company associates no longer on the scene I decided to try to promote the development of the emergency services in the UAE, where I was still regarded as of some value. I re-established my association with the UAE police directorate and found Colonel Shahab delighted to collaborate. I also contacted the university in Al-Ain where Dr Sadig was equally delighted to have my support and involvement. It was not easy to make progress from a distance, however, but I managed to visit from time to time by invitation from the police to their conferences and by teaching in the university during the vacations of the staff. Sadig had emerged as the leading academic authority in the Emirates on human factors associated with road traffic accidents and safety, and had obtained a big contract on the promotion of road safety for the UAE faculty from Monash University in Melbourne (backed by General Motors). Road traffic accidents were still ranked as the second most frequent cause of death in the UAE. With this money it was possible to establish a unit to research aspects of road safety including both road design and human factors. The severity of road trauma and its management was also measured. Unfortunately, Sadig did not have the support of a senior colleague on site, something that all new PhD research workers need if their ideas are not to be purloined by senior forces. I was not there and could not offer much support from a distance. Equally, I no longer had a post in the UAE university. The head of the Department of Engineering therefore took the grant over and the medical part was consigned to a subsidiary position. This was disappointing, but Sadig had done his best.

At this point I had a phone call that was very reminiscent of the call

I received from Colin Jones in the 1970s and which changed my life dramatically. It was from Alan Kennedy-Bolam, who was a director of Lancashire Ambulance Service NHS trust. He was interested in developing the emergency services of the UAE on behalf of the trust and asked if we could meet to discuss it. He duly arrived in Aberdeen and we met in the Royal Northern and University Club for dinner. As with my early meeting with Dr Colin Jones, Alan Kennedy-Bolam brought me out of retirement and back into the land of the living and my third career.

Alan was responsible for the promotion of emergency service development for his ambulance trust and had developed a vast external empire based on pre-hospital emergency care for the trust's training department. This included anything from first aid for industry through to the development of paramedic degree courses in association with the local university. Also included were consultancy services on emergency service development for overseas locations including Morocco, Pakistan and Brazil. He had been involved in the development of advanced human patient simulation techniques in Brazil and was an accomplished businessman. He had provided a very considerable annual income for the ambulance trust and had accumulated a vast number of national and international contacts over the years. I also had a large number of international associates but they were very different from Alan's. Equally, Alan's background was totally different from mine but we were both keen to promote pre-hospital health care in remote places, specifically in the Middle East. We therefore formed a partnership which developed into a company designed to promote the development of pre-hospital emergency care in the Middle East by training, consultancy and research. Alan was not much interested in research at that time but he soon saw its value in the promotion of the business. He carried out a consultancy study on the emergency services of Umm Al-Quwain in association with Dr Sadig's new centre at the university, but this was fraught with problems caused by the Egyptian engineering component. This was followed by a review of the Dubai emergency services carried out for the Dubai police ambulance service.

The Dubai police ambulance service was run by Major Mohammed Murad, an excellent and far sighted man. His main executive was Omer Sakaff, who had been a nurse on Das Island and had worked with me when training personnel on casualty handling during the Iran/Iraq war. He also came to the university and demonstrated ambulance and casualty handling techniques to the students. Sadig and I had ready access to the records for our epidemiological work and I gave development advice to the ambulance service to the extent that I was invited to become its medical director. The relationship was thus strong on both Alan's and my side but it was difficult to make much headway because we were not based in the UAE. There was little political support for British enterprises and Omer repeatedly stated that when a major contract was in the wind he had an immediate visit from the German, South African and Australian embassy. The British embassy was, however, conspicuous by its absence.

Since Alan had by now taken early retirement neither of us had an income, but our activities had to be funded. Without the support of a big organisation behind us this could be difficult to negotiate. Nevertheless, the future was gradually being defined and we decided to concentrate on the promotion of remote medicine internationally, from a UK base, with emphasis on emergency pre-hospital medicine.

At that juncture Alan contacted me to say that his associates in Brazil wanted to develop training for the oil company Petrobras and wished to visit Aberdeen to see how it was done. I was a bit concerned because I had not been involved for some time, and particularly when I found that they were coming during an Aberdeen holiday and that out of my former colleagues only Graham Page would be present. I dusted off my old slides and we hosted a meeting in the Accident and Emergency Department at Aberdeen Royal Infirmary. I had expected things to have moved on since my involvement and was surprised to find that not much had changed. The philosophy of remote health care and the system of medicine we had developed was still in existence. There were still problems with the rig medics not having professional status and in the recognition of military trained medics and their relationship with state registered nurses. Harry Horsley, now working from a post in the Faculty of Health and Social Care in RGU, had conducted an excellent study on the views, aspirations and problems of rig medics which set out many of the areas that needed attention. Principal among these were the need to review training schedules, the problem of professional isolation, the need to define the professional function of the medic and the problem of public protection in an unregulated professional group. This defined the problems which needed attention ten years previously and which were being actively addressed at that time by the RGIT offshore centre. The universities had now closed their offshore centres and training was carried out by a variety of organisations, some very good and some less good (according to medic feed-back). The academic co-ordinating function and professional development of the medic thus seemed to have frozen. Since 1989 the Health and Safety Executive had regulated training and set standards which medics needed to achieve for employment in the UK continental shelf. That was a big advance but it had not gone far enough. The closure of the university centres, however, had meant that the third essential component of the system – research – virtually ceased.

It was, however, gratifying to find that telemedicine had now caught on and its importance and use in general community medicine realised. The Scottish Office had established a study to determine the value of telemedicine operating from a central point in a main A&E department with peripheral general practitioner based units in the cottage hospitals of the north of Scotland. The study was based in the Accident and Emergency Department at Aberdeen Royal Infirmary with the clinical aspect under the management of James Ferguson. The design of the study and its evaluation was the responsibility of John Brebner in the university unit. This was a major research contract administered by the university and it brought both kudos and finance to the University of Aberdeen. It finally led to the establishment of the Scottish Centre for Telemedicine and Telehealth in Aberdeen with a large budget.

Probably the most impressive remote telemedical operator was Fiona Mair. In addition to her ability to manage clinical problems at a distance she had developed the medium for teaching to a high degree of sophistication and offered a variety of courses to remote places in association with Dr Colville Laird of Basics. The Brazillians were very impressed with this as was I. I was much less impressed, however, when I heard that Aberdeen university had decided to close the remote medicine unit in the Department of General Practice and Primary Care. They also decided to stop both research in telemedicine and the academic association with the UAE made possible by the provision of higher medical degrees. This seemed to be a retrograde step and was very disappointing. It was also difficult to understand because that unit was active in providing a continuing source of funds for the university in both research and educational development and cost nothing. Both the Brebners left the university at that time. They were disappointed but not too concerned because Eileen soon became president of the telemedicine section of the Royal Society of Medicine and John the treasurer. It was bad judgement by the university because within months of terminating work on telemedicine the Scottish Office finally decided that it should be developed and made a huge grant available for this purpose, which of course by-passed the university.

I could now see that the system of remote medicine which many of us in academe, industry and the community had worked so hard to research and establish was worth preserving and developing further from an Aberdeen base, involving those still around from the past but recruiting new blood to the cause so that the Aberdeen initiative should not be lost. The expertise and ambition shared by Alan and I was a good starting point since we had such different backgrounds, experience and skills. After much discussion we decided to establish a new academic institution to pick up the challenge and we named it the Institute of Remote Health Care. It was sad that the universities had not continued the development of this new form of health care – just at the time when its fundamental concepts were becoming so well recognised in the development of medicine for the following century. The trouble was that there was a considerable financial value to what had been achieved and the centres were sold off to fund other academic activities. The stated purpose of the new institute was the improvement of health care for those who live or work in remote places worldwide, while a secondary aim was the promotion of British medical education overseas. The second aim was based on the observation of the decline in British medical education in the Middle East.

The next step was to recruit a few like minded people to form the management group of the new institute, which was established as a company limited by guarantee. This meant that the group could not receive any remuneration. In spite of this recruitment was surprisingly easy and it was a bit like re-forming the fleet in the Napoleonic war after the failure of the treaty of Amiens in 1802. Many were from our past and initially some probably answered the call out of friendship and loyalty as well as interest. On my side Graham Page and Harry Horsley readily agreed to join as did John Smith (President of the Royal College of Surgeons of Edinburgh). Malcolm Valentine, who had carried out the basic epidemiological study of conditions requiring evacuation from offshore at RGIT, also agreed to join. He was now a distinguished GP with a powerful interest in continuing medical education and his presence was important.

On Alan's side Richard Fairhurst, who had been Medical Director of the Lancashire Ambulance Service and was now a director of standards for pre-hospital medicine at the Royal College of Surgeons of Edinburgh, joined. We also recruited Richard McLellen, who had taught in the desert with me and was a very effective teacher in RGIT. He now worked for BP. Both Sadig and Saleh Hussain joined. Ronald Ross, who had worked with me when we were both part of Sir Charles Illingworth's Department of Surgery in Glasgow and had become medical director of Healthcare International (a Glasgow hospital now owned by Abu Dhabi), also agreed to join the council. He was very supportive from the outset and became the treasurer. There was thus immediately a strong and very influential council, and as the new institute came into existence it had a group of prestigious and experienced council members to guide it. I was appointed as president and Alan as chief executive.

We decided that the new institute should be totally independent of external control, deriving its authority from the council. This was a most important principal even though there was no big organisation to support the early steps. Ordinary membership was to be restricted to those who had a proven record as reliable and well trained remote practitioners, with lesser grades of membership available for remote practitioners in training.

Our main attention was to be directed internationally but many members of the council felt that that a first project should be to investigate the situation in the North Sea. We had much background experience there, and after new lessons had been learned it would be easier to move on to the international scene. At this point Dr Mark Cheesman, a newly qualified occupational physician who had a real interest in the medicine of the UK continental shelf, got in touch. He had worked for several commercial providers of medical services for the offshore companies, knew the members of the current regulating bodies, had up to date knowledge of the scene and had just written a thesis on the epidemiology of illness and injury in the North Sea. This was an updated account of the initial study we carried out at RGIT many years before. He was therefore recruited to the council, and this completed the initial group.

Although there was now an enthusiastic new council for the new institute it was hampered by having no money. I had twice established an academic department from a standing start, however, so this was not too much of a worry. Alan and I turned to the Middle East and sought to raise funds for the initial establishment by providing consultancy advice and by training as before. In addition to the principle of independence we also took an early decision not to be involved in providing training and thus put ourselves in competition with training companies. We worked hard in the UAE and made just enough money to establish the institute by consultancy. We even obtained a contract to set up training for the staff of an airport but by the time we paid the company involved there was little left. Scottish Enterprise was asked for support but were of no help. Neither was the Department of Trade and Industry.

All this demonstrated that there were many opportunities for advancement in the UAE for UK academic authorities, but these were difficult to capitalise on with scant resources unless a bigger organisation could be involved. It thus seemed that in addition to a prestigious council to provide authority and guidance there was a need for an association with a major academic institution. I approached The Royal College of Surgeons of Edinburgh through John Smith and he was very supportive. He referred me to the Faculty of Pre-hospital Medicine (Richard Fairhurst's faculty), which was a good start. We needed a university, however, and so I wrote to Professor Mike Pitillo, Vice-chancellor of Robert Gordon University, and asked whether he would be interested in an association with the institute. The response was similar to that received from Dr Peter Clarke so many years before, which had led to the establishment of the very successful offshore medical centre. He was enthusiastic and I was introduced to Professor Valerie Maehle, Dean of the Faculty of Health and Social Care, whom I knew from the past. We signed an MoU between RGU and the institute and Professor Maehle became a member of the council.

Rapid progress was made as Professor David Rowley, Director of Education at the Edinburgh royal college, was enthusiastic about promoting his college in the UAE as well as developing an association with RGU. Richard Fairhurst also saw the benefits as his faculty had interests in rig medic education but was mainly only knowledgeable in emergency medicine. He was also keen on an association with RGU for the development of a possible degree course in pre-hospital trauma management.

We had been very impressed with the human simulator techniques established by Marcello Gloria in Brazil. This was computer controlled and could be used to train anybody from a first aider to medical students, nurses, paramedics, doctors and even trainee specialists preparing for higher diplomas and degrees. It seemed to be the way forward for practical training in medicine since it could provide practice in the practical management of emergencies without using patients. It was, however, very expensive and I felt that an attempt to introduce it would be more likely to succeed in the Middle East. We were already experienced in telemedicine and tele-education and the addition of simulation techniques seemed to complete the necessary technical armamentarium for remote education. On the advice of Dr Saleh Hussain I approached the Gulf Diagnostic Centre, run by Dr Khaddoura. It was a good establishment that had an excellent staff, was very well equipped, and had good associations for training with the police and the army. Dr Khaddoura was building an associated hospital and training centre but was also in advanced discussions with an American university. I got on very well with Dr Khaddoura but the association with the American university suggested that we were too late and we ran into commercial problems that required a greater financial commitment than we were able to make.

If the institute's main aim in the Middle East was to promote British medical education it seemed important to identify what the customers needed rather than to impose what already existed. I had many approaches over the years suggesting a need for support for local doctors aspiring towards the fellowship and membership examinations of the British royal colleges of medicine and surgery. I concluded that such support and training could be imported from UK by electronic means, which would save much expense and allow the trainees to remain in their local hospitals without re-locating to another country and culture. Equally, it would open up the market to those non-Emirate trainees who could not afford to give up their job and travel to Europe to attend courses.

I approached Dr BR Shetty, who had helped me fund the international journal of diabetes when I was its treasurer at the UAE University. He was in charge of a massive medical conglomerate called the New Medical Centre (NMC), which included several private hospitals, an ambulance service and a considerable pharmaceutical empire. He expressed interest in our project but said that we should get a move on because it was almost too late for the UK – everyone was now taking the American board exams. I immediately returned to Edinburgh and consulted John Smith. The college had just developed a course which seemed to fulfil the requirements but unfortunately it seemed too complicated to introduce to the Middle East, at least until further development. I therefore approached the Royal College of Physicians and Surgeons of Glasgow where the president, Ian Anderson, immediately warmed to the challenge and set up a group to determine the way forward. I returned to Dr Shetty who introduced me to the Vice-chancellor of the Higher Colleges of Technology, Dr Tayeb Kamali. His institution had a commercial wing called CERT and he proposed that the courses could be marketed through that medium. Between them they would be able to arrange the complex licensing arrangements needed by the Ministry of Health and the Ministry of Higher Education and Research. Dr Kamali showed me the facilities of CERT and they were indeed impressive. He had advanced tele-education equipment and was particularly proud of the simulation equipment he had for training oil companies drillers. I returned to Aberdeen very satisfied that the way forward in the Emirates had been identified. We had excellent academic bases for the promotion of our aims in both home and overseas locations, something which had been achieved in a remarkable short timescale. It would be wrong to assume that it had all been easy, however, for it had involved much 'blood, sweat and tears' and the expenditure of considerable personal funds by Alan and I. The associations from the past and our track record were of course vital.

Since we were standard setters, evaluators of courses and facilitators we had no clear product that could be marketed. Funding was almost entirely on the basis of membership fees. However, we had few members since we were not able to indicate the value of membership or even the existence of the institute. It was a bit of a chicken and egg situation. The first step seemed to be the establishment of a website which could be used not only to indicate what IRHC was all about but also to set up a means of communicating among members. There were many requests for information and extensive interest in the associated newsletter but few requests for membership from rig medics. Indeed, those which came were from doctors or providers of medical services in remote and hostile areas. It seemed that we had more interest from doctors and service providers than from our intended target of oil company medics!

Alan then suggested that we should have corporate membership for companies who had an interest in remote medicine provision and training. As this was rather a competitive business and the council was keen to remain strictly independent there was some discussion about the possibility of corporate members obtaining commercial advantages from membership. Care was taken to ensure that this did not happen but it did seem important that associated organisations working in the field should be able to know what the membership and council were thinking. Corporate membership was thus established. Equally, it seemed that the operators should be encouraged to state what they wished and be able to influence thinking in appropriate practical directions. I therefore contacted Dr Alistair Fraser and Dr Jonathan Ross, who had been successful members of BASMU in their early years and were now senior members of international Shell and British Gas medicine respectively. Both had training problems for their personnel in obscure and sometimes dangerous parts of the world. They could see that our approach on tele-education, association with both Royal colleges and universities and a broad based and prestigious council had value for their companies. They were invited to join the council and readily agreed. Shell also became a corporate member thereafter. Such organisations were thus more likely than academic outfits to understand that the services of a facilitator had a commercial value. It seemed that the funding problem was now on the way to achieving a solution also, which was just as well because both Alan and I were beginning to feel the pinch! The final requirement was to persuade a figure of high medical standing in the national scene to join and act as chairman. Sir Graeme Catto agreed to do this and that added the final accolade to the prestige of the new institute.

Meanwhile the council discussions largely centred around the problems of training, standards of remote practice and regulation of medics in the absence of registration. We tried to tackle the problem without offending existing official regulating and advisory bodies. Since the institute was relatively unknown it was important to determine that we were not just regarded as brash new boys but had genuine experience and knowledge which could be useful to the industry and the remote communities we were intent on serving. That is where independence was vital as was the absence of a competitive commercial base. It seemed that the way forward was to hold a symposium, ostensibly for members but also to invite representation from all those which had a possible interest in what we were endeavouring to achieve. Professor Maehle offered to sponsor the event and to host it in the conference facilities of the Department of Health and Social Care at RGU. This indicated the support and interest of RGU, which had been so involved in the developments of the past. Sir Graeme agreed to chair the symposium and I opened on the historical development of the institute and its current status. Malcolm Valentine gave a presentation on the new journal he had recently produced. Harry Horsley and Mark Cheesman spoke about their research studies on medic aspirations, reasons for evacuation from offshore structures, the need to improve both training and medical provision, and the re-establishment of research as a basis for advancing remote health care across the board. Richard Fairhurst recounted how he had been invited by the HSE to review the training standards required by statute and the results of his consultations, while Graham Page and Mark Mitchelson of the Accident and Emergency Department at Aberdeen Royal Infirmary described the present and past position of emergency evacuations from offshore.

We had wondered how many would turn up to the event but it was very well attended indeed, and when Sir Graeme conducted a full discussion to round things off it was clear that the new institute was welcomed by remote practitioners, training and medical service providers and the operators with universal support. An independent organisation was indeed required and not just for the support of the North Sea. In fact its importance to the international areas was even more welcomed. This single event established the new institute on a firm footing and after that it went from strength to strength. The support from corporate members and the website soon began to expand the ordinary membership and the financial situation improved even to the extent that the organisation was in a position to begin repaying the money loaned by Alan and I.

And so it was that a new and strong institute emerged in Aberdeen in a remarkably short timescale, using all the experience gained from previous organisations but with a strong international responsibility from the outset. It will be important to ensure that it is permanent this time, and that the initiative developed originally in Aberdeen in the 1970s is recognised not only as a medical development from Aberdeen, but one that has been contributed to by a wide range of academic, industrial and community agencies. It is likely to shape the form of medicine appropriate for succeeding generations – not only for the population of Great Britain but for all those who live and work in remote places associated with hazardous environments.

Acknowledgements

A LARGE NUMBER OF INDIVIDUALS AND ORGANISATIONS HAVE BEEN involved over the past thirty or forty years in the search for a system of remote medicine – most supportive of my efforts and some less so – but I acknowledge the contributions of them all. Most individuals have been mentioned throughout this book but some deserve special mention and thanks. The late Dr Colin Jones of British Petroleum was the co-founder of the original Institute of Offshore and Environmental Medicine with me and without his drive it would not have happened. Dr John A Brebner soon became my partner, colleague and close friend throughout the difficult birth of the concept and he deserves special credit for his persistence, wisdom and judgement. Other close and loyal adherents to the cause who contributed strongly to the development of remote health care through thick and thin include Professor Graham Page, Dr Peter Clarke, Principal of RGIT, Vice-Admiral Sir John Rawlins, Dr RM Laws, Director of the British Antarctic Survey, the late Mr Eric Salmon, Dr Graeme Nicol and the late Dr William Leese of Mobil. In the final phase of the saga, namely the emergence of the Institute of Remote Health Care, Mr Alan Kennedy-Bolam, its co-founder and chief executive, has been tireless in his endeavours on the development of this institute.

Above all I would not have been able to continue into the time of 'The sear and the yellow leaf' without the constant support and help of my wife Morag and my daughter Sarah-Jane, and I owe them both a debt of gratitude. In writing the book I have had continuing excellent advice from my editor Mr Duncan Lockerbie. The Press and Journal has reported on the development of offshore and remote medicine faithfully over the years since the establishment of the offshore industry in the North Sea and it has photographed the key events - even climbing Morrone to record the opening of the laboratory there - and the establishment of the British Antarctic Survey Medical Unit at the Centre for Offshore Health, RGIT. I am most grateful to Mr Alan Scott of the Press and Journal for allowing me to reproduce many of these illustrations, as I am to Alistair Fraser for the use of his photograph as the cover image.

LIST OF PUBLISHED WORK

Oliver E, Miller JDB and Norman JN (1978)
Steriods and secondary drowning. Lancet 105–106

Auld CD, Light IM and Norman JN (1979)
Accidental hypothermia and rewarming in dogs. Clin Sci 56: 601–606

**Norman JN, Childs CM, Jones C, Smith JAR, Ross JAS, Riddle G,
MacKintosh A, McKie NIP, Macaulay II and Fructus X (1979)**
Management of a complex diving accident. Undersea Biomed Res
6: 209–216

Leese WLB and Norman JN (1979)
*Helicopter passenger survival suit standards in the UK offshore oil
industry.* Aviat Space and Environ Med 50: 110–114

Smith JAR and Norman JN (1979)
Volume infusion in experimental refractory shock. Brit J Surg 66: 80–83

Smith JAR and Norman JN (1979)
Use of glucocorticoids in refractory shock. Surgery Vol 149: 369–373

Smith JAR and Norman JN (1979)
The nature and therapy of refractory shock. Injury 10: 269–296

Light IM, McKerrow W and Norman JN (1980)
Immersion coveralls for use by helicopter passengers. J Soc Occup Med
30: 141–148

Light IM and Norman JN (1980)
The thermal properties of a survival bag incorporating metallised plastic sheeting. Aviat Space Environ Med 51: 367

Light IM, White MA, Allan D and Norman JN (1980)
Thermal balance in divers. Lancet 1: 1362

Auld CD, Light IM and Norman JN (1980)
Cooling responses in shivering and non-shivering dogs during induced hypothermia. Cli Sci 58: 501

Light IM, Dingwall RHM and Norman JN (1980)
The thermal protection offered by lightweight survival systems. Aviat Space Environ Med 51: 1100–1103

Light IM and Norman JN (1980)
Rewarming from hypothermia in remote locations. Aberdeen Postgraduate Medical Bulletin 14: 9–11

Norman JN (1981)
The Institute of Environmental and Offshore Medicine. The Aberdeen University Review 49: 1–7

Smith JAR and Norman JN (1982)
The fluid of choice for resuscitation of severe shock. Br J Surg Vol 69: 702–705

Norman JN and Brebner JA (1983)
Diving medicine in the Middle East. Postgraduate Doctor (Middle East) 6: 311–314

Norman JN and Brebner JA (1983)
Hypothermia in the elderly. Current Practice 47: 16–17

Light IM, Norman JN and Stoddart M (1983)
Rewarming from immersion hypothermia: reduction of afterdrop. Scot Med J 28: 80–81

Norman JN (1984)
The problems of the hazardous environment. Clinical Research Reviews
    4: 161–162

Norman JN (1985)
Work in cold climates. Travel Medicine International 3(4): 194–196

Norman JN (1986)
Work in cold climates. International Journal of Environmental Studies
    26: 329–340

Norman JN and Brebner JA (1987)
*The development of an occupational health service for the British
    Antarctic Survey.* Arctic Medical Research 45: 55

**Norman JN, Ballantine BN, Brebner JA, Brown B, Gauld SJ, Mawdsley J,
    Roythorne C, Valentine MJ and Wilcock SE (1988)**
Medical evacuations from offshore structures. Br J Indust Med
    45: 619–623

Norman JN and Laws RM (1988)
Remote health care for Antarctica: the BAS Medical Unit. Polar Record
    24: 317–320

Norman JN and Brebner JA (1988)
Remote medicine. Occupational Health 40: 598–600

Norman JN and Brebner JA (1988)
Occupational health care in the Antarctic. Occupational Health
    40: 602–604

Norman JN and Brebner JA (1988)
Health care for divers. Occupational Health 40: 605–608

Norman JN and Brebner JA (1988)
Environmental heat. Occupational Health 40: 609–612

Norman JN (1989)
*Medical care and human biological research in the British Antarctic
    Survey Medical Unit.* Arctic Medical Research 48: 103–116

Norman JN, Brebner JA and Ruddiman RA (1991)
Study on dental care requirements for EMSI. Report to European Space
Agency No 9143/90/F/BZ

Norman JN, MacLean R and Haston W (1993)
Teleremsi: telemedicine at a real remote site. Report to European Space
Agency No TBD 92

Maclean JR, Brebner JA and Norman JN (1995)
A review of Scottish telemedicine. Journal of Telemedicine and Telecare
1: 1–6

Brebner JA, Norman JN, Page JG and Ruddick-Brackon H (1995)
Research based training for the nurse practitioner. Accident and
Emergency Nursing 3: 92–94

**Norman JN, Brebner JA, Brebner, EM, Lloyd OL, Ruddick-Brackon H,
Ahmed, M El Sadig H, Catto GRD, and Ledingham I (1995)**
Telematics in undergraduate teaching. Medical Education 29: 403–406

Brebner JA, Ruddick-Brackon H, Norman JN, and Page JG (1996)
The nurse practitioner – management of minor trauma. Accident and
Emegency Nursing 4: 43–46

**Brebner EM, Brebner JA, Norman JN, Brown PAJ, Ruddick-Brackon H,
Lanphear J (1997)**
Intercontinental postmortem studies using interactive television. Journal
of Telemedicine and Telecare 3: 48–52

Gomes J, Lloyd O, Revitt DM and Norman JN (1997)
Erythrocyte cholinesterase activity levels in desert farm workers. J Occup
Med 47: 90–94

**Norman JN, Brebner JA, Brebner Eileen, Ruddick-Brackon H, McIlvenny S
and Sim AJW (1997)**
International telemedicine. Journal of Telemedicine and Telecare 3: 1–2

Norman JN and Gomes J (1997)
Occupational medicine in the United Arab Emirates. Emirates Medical
Journal 15: 3–4

Norman JN, Al-Hassani, Brebner JA and Bener A (1997)
First-aid knowledge – an international comparison. Kuwait Med J
29: 407–412

**Brebner EM, Brebner JA, Norman JN, Brown PAJ, Ruddick-Brackon H and
Lanphear JH (1997)**
A pilot study in medical education using interactive television. Journal of
Telemedicine and Telecare 3 Supplement 1: 10–12

**Brebner EM, Brebner JA, Norman JN, Brown PA, Ruddick-Brackon H and
Lanphear JH (1997)**
Intercontinental postmortem studies using interactive video. Journal of
Telemedicine and Telecare 3: 48–52

Bener A, Norman JN, Brebner JA, Achan NV and Al-Falsi AS (1998)
*Asthma associated with road traffic accidents in the United Arab
Emirates.* J Traffic Med 26: 109–114

Brebner EM, Brebner JA, Ruddick-Brackon H and Norman JN (1998)
*The development of a telemedicine laboratory as a medical faculty
resource.* Journal of Telemedicine and Telecare 4 supplement 1: 29–30

**Norman JN, Brebner JA, Ruddick-Brackon H, Brebner EM and
Al-Ozairi SS (1998)**
*International collaboration in the development of post-graduate research
training.* Medical Education 32: 82–84

Norman JN (2000)
Telemedicine. Kuwait Medical Journal 32: 3–4

**Al-Maskeri F, Bener A, Al-Kaabi A, Al-Suwaidi N, Norman JN and
Brebner JA (2000)**
*Asthma and respiratory symptoms among school children in United Arab
Emirates.* Allergie & Immunologie 32: 159–163

Al-Ahwal SH, Norman JN and Brebner JA (2000)
Heat cramps in a hot desert work-site. Kuwait Medical Journal 32: 382–386

Gomes J, Lloyd OL, Norman JN and Pahwa P (2001)
*Dust exposure and impairment of lung function at a small iron foundry
in a rapidly developing country.* Occup Environ Med 58: 656–662

Norman JN and Alsajir MB (2001)
Tele-education – postgraduate education. Med Principles Pract
10: 115-122

El-Sadig HA, Norman JN, Lloyd OL, Romilly P and Bener A (2002)
*Road traffic accidents in the United Arab Emirates: trends of morbidity
and mortality during 1977-1998.* Accident Analysis and Prevention
34: 465–476

Al Maskari F, El Sadig M and Norman, JN (2007)
*The prevalence of macrovascular complications among diabetic patients
in the United Arab Emirates.* Cardiovascular Diabetology 6: 24

Norman, JN (2010)
Remote health care: ready to go global. Surgeon's news 9: 50–51

Chapters in Books

Norman JN (1979)
The case for a mobile intensive care unit. Medical Aspects of Diving
Accidents. Commission of the European Communities: Luxembourg/
Kirschberg

Childs CM and Norman JN (1979)
Loss of consciousness in divers. Hyperbaric Medicine Ed. Smith G.
pp 373–376 Aberdeen University Press: Aberdeen

Norman JN (1979)
A review of neurological decompression sickness. Hyperbaric Medicine Ed.
Smith G. pp 352–356 Aberdeen University Press: Aberdeen

Norman JN and Leese WLB (1981)
Diving medicine. Thoracic Medicine Ed. Emerson P.
pp 527–532 Butterworths: London

Norman JN (1981)
Medical care in the Antarctic. Circumpolar Health 1981: Proceedings of 5th
Internat Symposium on Circumpolar Health Ed. Harvald B and Hansen
JPH. pp 74–76 Nordic Council for Arctic Medical Research.

Norman JN (1984)
Medical support for diving operations. Proceedings of 7th Internat
Conference on Hyperbaric Oxygen. Moscow

Norman JN (1984)
The management of intercurrent illness in deep saturation diving.
Proceedings of 7th Internat Conference on Hyperbaric Oxygen. Moscow

Norman JN (1996)
First aid and management of blast injury. Guidelines for the Safe Use of
Explosives Underwater Ed. Barrett RW. pp 54–58 Marine Technology
Directorate Report 96/01

Books

Norman JN and Brebner JA (1985)
The Offshore Health Handbook. Martin Dunitz Ltd: London

Brebner JA and Norman JN (1988)
Audio-visual Immediate Care Package in Arabic. RGIT Publ.

Milne AH, Norman JN, Brebner JA, Johnson IWB (1988)
British Antarctic Survey Medical Manual. NERC: Swindon

Norman JN and El Sadig HA (1996)
Emergency First Aid. (Arabic version) Silver Information Service: Cairo.
ISBN 977-5709-05-9

Norman JN, Al-Masabi SH, El-Sadig M and Haj AM (2004)
Emergency First-aid for Industrial and Remote Settings. Trafford: Victoria
Canada. ISBN 1-4120-2620-2

Norman, JN (2009)
In Search of A Penguin's Egg. Author House. ISBN 978-1-4490-1729-3

INDEX

Dundee, University of 27, 44;
Dundee, University of Abertay 134;
Dyce 31, 54, 55;

E

Edholm, Otto (Prof) 59, 60, 67;
Edinburgh 44, 45, 148;
    New St Andrew's House 44;
    Shell House (Herriot Row) 44;
Edinburgh, Duke of 73;
Edinburgh, University of 20, 43;
Elliott, David (Commander) 19,
    34, 36, 40, 41, 42, 43, 44, 46, 47,
    48, 50;
El-Sadig, Mohammed 132, 133,
    134, 135, 136, 137, 140, 141, 142,
    145;
Energy, Department of 24, 27, 48,
    51, 56, 92;
Esso 27, 29, 30;
European Economic Community
    139;
European Space Agency (ESA) 120;

F

Fairhurst, Richard (Dr) 145, 146,
    147, 150;
Falconer, Dale 43;
Falkland Islands 19, 66, 102, 103;
    Port Stanley 19, 66, 98, 102, 103;
Farquharson, Captain 71, 74;
Ferguson, James (Dr) 143;
Foresterhill College of Nursing 61,
    92;

Fort William 48;
France 117;
Fraser, Alistair (Dr) 68, 102, 149;
Freeland, Bill (Dr) 67, 68;
Fructus, Xavier (Dr) 39–40, 48;
Fuchs, Vivian (Sir) 60;

G

Gaelic Healthguard 33, 64;
Gallerne, Andre 52, 53, 54;
Garner, Tony (Dr) 77;
Gaskin, Max (Prof) 29;
Gauld, Stuart 92;
General Medical Council 127;
Gilbert, Mike (Dr) 78, 79, 80, 82;
Gillanders, Lewis (Prof) 118, 124;
Girton College 100, 101, 118;
Glasgow 28, 69, 98, 131, 145;
Glasgow, University of 16, 27, 88;
Gloria, Marcello 147;
Golden, Frank (Commander) 47;
Goldsmith, Rainer (Prof) 60;
Grampian Health Board 25, 53, 114;
Grand, Fleming (Dr) 136;
Great Yarmouth 32, 34, 35, 42;
Gulf Diagnostic Centre 147;

H

Hadley, Donald (Dr) 66, 67, 85;
Halley (Antarctic) 98, 108;
Halley Bay 16;
Hampstead 59, 69;
Harvey, Derek (Dr) 93, 115, 116;
Hastings, Robin (Dr) 92;

Haston, Wendy (Dr) 117;
Health and Safety Commission 27;
Health and Safety Executive 92,
  118, 143;
Healthcare International 145;
Home and Health Department 27,
  32, 44;
Home Office 27;
Horsley, Harry 113, 142, 145, 150;
House, Mary 83;
House, Max (Prof) 83, 84, 118;
Houston, Ronnie (Dr) 19, 21, 30,
  34, 41, 43, 44, 56;
Howie, Bruce (Dr) 25, 53, 114;
Hughes, John 30, 32, 34, 35, 36, 99;

I

Illingworth, Charles (Sir) 145;
Institute of Environmental and
  Offshore Medicine 28, 43, 53,
  57, 58, 99, 117;
  Disbanding 89;
  Foundation of 21–22, 23–24;
  Independence from the
    Department of Surgery 62–65;
  Medical Service 24, 58–59, 76, 86;
  Relationship with BAS 66–69, 89;
  Relationship with OMS 57–59, 65,
    86, 88;
  Research 39, 41, 48–51, 53, 54, 58,
    59, 60, 68–69, 73–74, 76, 85–86,
    87;
  Training 27, 46–48, 58, 60–62, 64,
    67–68, 75–77, 81–83, 85, 86;
Institute of Naval Medicine 33, 34,
  43, 46, 47;

Institute of Remote Health Care. *See
  herein* Norman, Nelson (Prof);
International Antarctic Science
  Group (SCAR) 117;
Irvine, Maxwell (Prof) 122, 129;

J

Johnson, Chris (Dr) 85, 107;
Johnson, Derek (Dr) 47;
Johnson, Ian 61, 68, 76, 81, 88, 92;
Jones, Colin (Dr) 16, 17–19, 20, 21,
  22, 23, 24, 25, 27–30, 36, 39, 40,
  41, 42, 43, 44, 49, 50, 52–53, 72,
  86, 141;

K

Kamali, Tayeb (Dr) 148;
Kennedy-Bolam, Alan 141, 142,
  144, 145, 146, 148, 149, 150, 151;
Kennedy, David (Dr) 113;
Kepplestone Mansion 76, 85, 88,
  91, 94, 101, 110, 111;
Khartoum, University of 133;
Kimsit, Maida (Dr) 51;
Krickler, Steve (Dr) 107;
Kuwait 123, 124, 126;

L

Laird, Colville (Dr) 143;
Lancashire Ambulance Service
  141, 145;
Laws, Dick (Dr) 67, 69, 89, 90, 94,
  100, 105;